A Little More Time

First published in the United Kingdom by
Porto Publishing March 2007

Porto Publishing
59 The Avenue
Ealing
London
W13 8JR

www.portopublishing.com

A CIP catalogue record for this book is available from the British Library, London.

Typesetting and Design by Porto Publishing

Printed and bound in Great Britain by
Bookforce UK Ltd

ISBN 13: 978-1-905930-02-9

A Little More Time

Margaret Hurdman

Contents

Illustrations

Acknowledgements

I must admit there were times when I thought this book would never be finished, and

I would like to thank all who have assisted me in producing 'A Little More Time'.

It has been made possible most of all by my tolerant husband John and my family, to whom I owe so much for putting up with a scatterbrained mother!

My special friends who have helped me: Alwena, Lesley, Nancy, Brenda and Jim.

Particular thanks to Christine, my editor, and Alan, for they have brought the entire book to fruition.

Also for the support of all the people who believe in me.

Most of all, my gratitude to Abe, my guide and constant friend, who has made all things possible.

Introduction

A Little more Time

Margaret Hurdman

Margaret Hurdman is an International Medium with over thirty years experience in the field of conversing with spirit. Whilst undergoing open heart surgery in 1974, Margaret was pronounced dead on three separate occasions, twice in the operating theatre and once in the recovery room. During these episodes she received a glimpse of the spirit world, and met with her son and other deceased members of her family. It was these near death experiences that eventually led her to realise her purpose in life was to work solely for spirit. Since that time she has devoted her life using the many facets of her remarkable gift. Her clarity of insight coupled with her amazing ability to channel evidence from the spirit world has brought her recognition as a brilliant Medium. As president of the Rhyl, North Wales, SNU (Spiritualist National Union) church, her passion for charity work is legendary in her local community.
In constant demand for stage, television and radio appearances, she is devoted to all aspects of her work.

Her second manuscript has been a work in progress following an unexpected level of interest created by her self published autobiography 'Margaret – The Person'. Born in the Midlands, Margaret moved to North Wales where she continues to live with her extended family. 2006 saw the celebration of her fiftieth wedding anniversary to her beloved husband John. With a grown family of her own, Margaret understands the problems of every day life. Approachable and down to earth, her working class roots remain evident. First appearances might suggest that Margaret was just an ordinary woman leading a very ordinary life. Those who have benefited from her vast knowledge and ability would suggest otherwise.

Very few women of her age could sustain such a demanding schedule. Her thirst for her work is insatiable. Her career expands constantly with a host of public appearances; demonstrations in Wales, Manchester, Liverpool and Devon, with repeat trips to the Channel Islands, Ireland, Europe and the United States of America.

In today's world of self indulgence and monetary gain, her refreshing attitude to life and her work allows her to cut across all boundaries of colour, creed and race. It is for this very reason that she has been encouraged to share her experiences.

Chapter
1

Spiritual Awakening

I have been asked many times to talk at length about my near death experiences. In total, I have almost passed to Spirit on three separate occasions. These occasions have ultimately changed every aspect of my life.

One of my first memories was being woken on the hospital ward before my first operation. I was encouraged to eat breakfast, a serving of tea and toast. At three o' clock in the morning, and barely conscious, it was no wonder I had no appetite. Surgery procedure has certainly changed over the years! As I was being transferred to the operating theatre, mixed emotions and concerns for my family were uppermost in my mind. *Had I told my boys how much I loved them? Would John be able to cope without me? Memories of my parents' anguished expressions as they tried desperately to hide their fears.*

I felt strangely detached; the pre-med had no doubt taken effect! That morning I had concerned myself with irrelevant details; I distinctly recall requesting that no one be allowed to see me without my artificial eye. I fretted excessively about waking with tubes protruding from my nose, all no doubt masking my real fear of whether I would wake at all. As I approached the main theatre doors the anaesthetist was waiting to greet me; he had a gentle reassuring manner. The surgeon stood behind him smiling, projecting an air of confidence as he set about his duties. I remember little more until I found myself looking down on my body. I could see the doctors working intensely, and I could hear the sounds of the machines. Then I found myself in a tunnel; a sense of amazement encompassed every part of me. I appeared to be moving at a terrific speed, yet I felt no fear. As I started to slow down I noticed a bright light, as I moved closer to the light, its brightness emanated in every direction. Directly in front of me stood two people, an elderly lady, who appeared strangely familiar, was holding the arm of a young boy. As I looked closer it soon became apparent that the lady was indeed my special Gran. She smiled and said they were fine but they were not ready for me. The young boy radiated such warmth as he spoke, “Hello Mum, I’m Jonathan”, the sound of which I can hear with total clarity to this very day. I stood transfixed as my Gran promptly reminded me that I had to go back, my boys needed me.

That instant I was returned to my body, and from that moment on my life was never to be the same. During the same operation I left my body for a second time, I remember very clearly looking down on my body and thinking *what a bloody mess!* Machines and tubes were everywhere, I seemed to be getting a lot of attention. At this point I felt myself travelling back through a tunnel. It felt like I was inside a kaleidoscope travelling at a terrific speed. I was surrounded by the most beautiful colours heading towards a white light which grew with intensity the closer I got to it. I was met by what I now know to be my primary guide, the Spirit guide who walks beside me throughout my lifetime. I asked him who he was and he replied, *“Call me as you will”*. I have since referred to him as Abe and I have been aware of his presence ever since.

We all have many guides who change depending on our needs and purpose, but our primary guide remains with us from our birth until we return to Spirit. Abe then went on to explain that it was not my time and that I must return. I distinctly remember him saying *"Return my daughter, this is not your time"*. My next impression was being back in the intensive care unit. I could see three other patients none of whom appeared to be fully dressed.

My husband John was sitting beside my bed he was wearing a shirt I had never liked. Despite being very aware of my surroundings no one seemed to realise my presence. I could not understand why John was so upset, he was telling me things he might not otherwise have mentioned. The nurse was telling him that they could do no more to help me; I heard the nurse's words as she told John I was going. *Going where?* I thought. I had no intention of leaving his side. Instantly, I was enveloped in an illuminating light. An image appeared before me, my special friend Abe. I was told quite categorically that I must return, I remember his words so clearly, *"My beloved daughter, if you come any closer you can not go back, our plan for you is to work for Spirit"*. Again he re-iterated that I must return stating, *"When the time is right and only then we will come for you, not one moment before or after, go back my beloved daughter, all is well. I will never leave you, I will be with you until the end of your life"*.

I remember an intense sensation of love, trust and belonging. The desire to remain was overwhelming, but the love for my family pulled me back to my body. After all I had a wonderful husband, three beautiful sons and loving parents. The amazing colours and the feeling of peace and serenity will always remain with me. All fear of death totally dissolved. It was almost two weeks later before I found myself back in the ward, now a very different person; confused, but a person with a purpose. It was to take a further twelve years before I became fully aware of what this purpose involved. Up until that point I had no particular direction, and with only a basic education my grasp of the situation was nominal. My fear of madness was tangible, yet as my development progressed, my fears subsided. One of the most memorable moments of my life was the sense of relief when I finally came to realise the reality of Spirit. To that end I have dedicated my life to help others understand that our loved ones are merely a thought away, that death is a natural progress and that the ties of love are never broken.

I am driven to pass on the knowledge with which I was entrusted and by doing so eliminate the fear of death and pain of bereavement. Over thirty years have now passed since those fateful experiences. The impact of meeting with my son and gran remains as vivid today as it has always been. Jonathan was our first born son - many people will be able to identify with me when I say that the passing of our much awaited baby was such a harrowing experience I simply survived in what I can only describe as a living torment. There appeared no reason for his passing and I was left a very bitter woman. I felt that I had failed everybody; I never held him in my arms, never was I allowed what every mother dreams of, to have touched his face and felt the warmth of his body. After his birth I was very ill, and all the arrangements for his funeral were made by my husband. I had no recollection of naming our son. It was only much later, fourteen years to be precise, when I was recovering from my heart surgery that I was discussing my near death experiences with John, when he immediately disappeared into the attic and returned with a box containing all our legal papers. As I unfolded a document I was surprised to discover that the name of Jonathan Hurdman was attributed to our son. There in black and white was confirmation that baby Jonathan was certified stillborn. My husband had chosen his name and in an attempt to cope with our anguish we buried our heads and never spoke of our loss. Now it is though he has never gone away as I see him frequently and also other people I have loved who have since passed on to a higher level. My dad in particular has always been close by, a tower of strength both in this life and the next. My mother still has the ability to express her displeasure when at times I behave in a manner she wouldn't approve of. As always when I sense their presence I can smell the familiar aroma of their favourite Players cigarettes.

I have been blessed with many wonderful memories. I have been fortunate to meet countless individuals from all walks of life and formed life long friendships with people I would never have met had my life not taken such an unusual direction. It has not always been an easy choice; a medium's life has an abundance of drawbacks. Sometimes the burdens of others and the worries that they bring weigh heavily on your shoulders. It has not always been easy to maintain my own space and individuality, but the draw to continue with my work is overwhelming. My rather hectic schedule was recently disrupted when I discovered in January 2006 that a malignant tumour had formed on one of my kidneys. Only a few months later I am recovering at home following a series of successful operations. What better time to initiate my desire to complete my second manuscript!

My Spiritual development has always remained my main focus, the concept of putting my experiences to paper never crossed my mind until it became apparent from the people I have met that there was an increasingly desperate need for Spiritual enlightenment. An unexpected level of interest created by my self-published autobiography has encouraged me to create a reference that could prove beneficial to all those who seek a greater understanding.

Surprisingly, one of the first lessons I learnt was that not all Spiritualists are Spiritually minded! I was shocked at the level of jealousy and the frustration of needing to develop your abilities in an atmosphere of negativity. Had I myself taken to heart what two other mediums told me in my early days of development, I would have given up there and then. I stood in awe of the big names of medium-ship until I visited a very renowned place of learning. I decided to book a sitting with what I believed was a top class medium. I paid my £15.00 fee, which was a considerable amount of money to spare at that time. As I was looking forward, in anticipation of my future work, I thought that if it gave me greater direction then it would be worth it.

I entered the room where the medium was seated; she invited me to join her then looked at me so intensely I began to feel quite uncomfortable. My initial instinct was that I must have looked as nervous as I felt. She began the sitting by informing me that she could see Spirit working with me and that they were praising my work. I was delighted but then she went on to add,
"Yes my dear you will work for Spirit, but you will always be a back ground worker, a lady to be relied on to make the tea, arrange the flowers, and be there when needed. You are however too shy and too quiet and I do feel you will never do platform work".
She asked me what my aim was; I replied that I would like to teach medium-ship, to demonstrate and to be able to prove survival without any room for doubt. When she asked me what experience I had, I informed her that I had been a vice president for two years and a president of a Spiritualist National Union church for a further two years. In addition I also worked on platform. She looked at me with total disbelief and made a rather feeble excuse that she must not have been in tune that day mainly due to being overtired. Ironically, eight years later I stood in at a very large venue for that very same medium when she was unable to work due to illness. What a waste of £15.00!

On another occasion I went to a demonstration with a group of friends in a small private hotel. The medium entered the room as if he were royalty; all that was missing was the royal wave. He immediately approached me and said he wished to talk to me about my husband in the Spirit world. I said *"I think not my friend"*, to which he replied *"I mean you the lady in the blue jumper"*. It was definitely me he wished to speak with and he continued to tell me that my husband needed me to know that I should get on with my life, as I had a lot of living to do and a lot of loving to give. I sat there with my mouth wide open. I answered that I was sorry but he had the wrong person. He wasn't amused and asked if I was blocking him. *"Indeed not"*, I answered. *"Then what is it you don't understand?"* was his reply. I pointed out that my husband was alive and well and that I had left him washing up at the sink that morning. The medium was furious and accused me once again of blocking him, stating that my energy contradicted his.

It was probably the first time I had realised just how responsible my work was to be. I was mindful of the people who could have easily been hurt and the bad feeling the medium could have created towards the Spiritualism movement. Responsibility is an essential commodity; yes, it is possible to be mistaken, and sometimes the messages do go to the wrong people. Better to admit the mistake than to fantasise and bluff. Had I been someone whose husband had passed, I would have been hanging onto every word; but what of the truth and what about the heartache that could have been caused? A responsible medium is concerned with conveying *only* that which is provided by Spirit.

The following chapters will endeavour to highlight various aspects of medium-ship. Have no doubt there is a lot to learn, but for all those who choose to tread this path, there is much Spiritual reward.

Chapter
2

Formative Years

I was blessed with a happy childhood and loving parents. One of my happiest memories was when I was seven years old. I was recovering from an operation and I remember quite clearly my dad taking me out for the day. In those days my dad drove a large lorry; we were carrying 'shoddy fluff waste', as the town's main employers were carpet manufacturers. We started out very early in the morning, we were on the road by half past five. I remember it being such a thrill sitting beside my dad high up in the cab. We stopped after a few hours at a road side café and bought steaming hot cups of tea and bacon sandwiches. Dad would put the sandwiches under the hood of the engine to keep them warm until we were ready to eat them. When we reached the factory the ladies were looking out for me. I was very spoiled; there were sweets, cuddles and smiles. Maybe they felt sorry for me - a child with a bandaged eye must have touched their hearts. I visited on many other occasions and never came away from that factory without a bag of sweets and all sorts of goodies. The foreman always managed to find something special for me, such as crayons or colouring pencils. It was having my dad all to myself that made the memories so special. The love and respect I had for my dad have remained with me throughout my life. My dad was not a posh fella or the Brain of Britain but he could make me smile and laugh like no one else could. He would brighten up my day simply knowing he was there.

Another special memory was watching my mum and dad dancing; sometimes it would be olde time dancing, on other occasions it might be modern or ballroom. They were both very good dancers, and I can remember my mum making me a little dance dress out of silk she bought from a rummage sale. We got by because they used whatever they could lay their hands on. My dad had a rare sense of humour, he often used to go to the rubbish skips at night and inevitably came back with something he could make use of.

I remember playing whist with my parents. When I was about ten years old we won first prize, it was a Christmas turkey. We felt as if we had won the pools. The tickets were only about a shilling (five pence) and that included a cup of tea and biscuits. Eventually the interest in whist began to decline so we joined everyone else to play bingo. I recall the anticipation of mum or dad waiting for just one number; dad would be saying under his breath, *'pull the bugger'*. We never got rich playing whist and we never got rich playing bingo, but we certainly became rich with our companions.

My granny was a good medium; her front room was a stopping off point for the neighbours. Granny's mates used to call on a Saturday night when all the men were at the pub. If one of them had baked we had cakes and tea. The house was always full of laughter. I always hid under the table where the chenille table cloth touched the floor. Every year granny would make all the men hand knitted socks and the ladies home made toffee. My father always struggled into the socks that rarely fitted and made his feet itch, but he would never tell her as she would have sat for hours knitting those socks. I still have a vivid memory of her sitting there with her glasses on the end of her nose. My gran was the kindest soul you could meet and I remember very clearly the wonderful days of my childhood spent with her and my Aunty Alice. I don't remember much of my granddad, except for the fact he was very short in height and liked a pint. When he'd had a few pints his mood would change and he would become quite cantankerous. He was a difficult man to get close to, but he also had a heart. He used to grow prize chrysanthemums and one day I unwittingly picked them. My gran did not know how to tell him, yet he didn't even blink and took them from me as if I had presented him with a special present. I believe he could be quite a bully, in his younger days he was considered a bit of a rogue and jumped ship. He was always out to make a quick buck.

On one occasion he overheard his mates talking in the pub, they were discussing where to deposit a sack. With his mind working overtime he assumed the sack would contain something of worth such as a lamb or a pig that could be sold on the black market. He was waiting at the entrance and as soon as the sack was left unattended he grabbed it and escaped over the fence eager to get home and check out his catch. On arrival home he discovered the contents of the sack was just a dead dog that was to be buried and he had to return it to the pub.

One of my most treasured memories of gran and granddad was spending Sunday afternoons with them when they played the piano. On top of the piano was a blue and white bottle containing milk of magnesia. Despite the disgusting taste I was always beside my granddad waiting for my spoonful, it made me feel close to him, as I felt included. On the day of granddad's funeral, he was laid out in the front room, I wasn't allowed to go in the room but gran asked me to go up stairs and asked me to fetch a clean cloth. As I was coming back down the stairs I asked my gran why granddad was asleep in the back room. My gran and mum gasped as I could not have known that granddad had died; I sometimes wonder if that was the first sign of my awareness. I have spoken about my mum's parents but I know very little about my dad's. His parents both died when he was an infant and he was raised by his sister. I understand my paternal grandfather was a master builder and he played a big part in the building of Saint Mary's Church in Kidderminster. I regret not finding out more sooner, as now it is too late to make enquiries.

My first memory was when I was two years of age. I was travelling to Hull with my mum and Auntie Alice; we were sitting in a train that had no corridor and my mum was desperate to go to the loo. Eventually she resorted to peeing in her rain hat, opening the window with the leather sash and being shocked when the wind blew the contents right back and hit her in her face. We were on our way to see my dad, who was due to embark with my Uncle Sid. Another early recollection occurred when I was about four years old. I had seen many specialists about my eye, but on this occasion I can remember kicking up quite a fuss, so that I had to be chloroformed before they could examine me. To this day I am unable to stand anything covering my face. I visited the hospital on a regular basis; Mum used to bribe me to be good by promising chips and mushy peas in the café, and if I was especially good we would have hot chestnuts from the barrowman on the way home.

Throughout my life family have played a central role in every part of my life. Having recently celebrated our fiftieth wedding anniversary I could never have imagined on the night I went to a dance hall and met John for the first time that we would still be together all these years later. I was sixteen and had gone to the dance with another fella. John asked me to dance, and I was instantly struck by the fact he was so good looking; he had just returned from abroad and had a deep tan. I remember thinking he was quite arrogant at first, but I was already smitten. When he asked me to meet him the following evening, I accepted, even though I had already made arrangements to meet the date I had arrived at the dance with. We met at the cinema, and our relationship flourished, and we were married when I was eighteen.

We are as different as chalk and cheese, but it is true that opposites attract. During the first six weeks of knowing each other we argued constantly, now fifty years have passed and I wouldn't change a moment. It was a beautiful frosty day and the wedding was done on a shoestring. I remember my dad saying to me that it was not too late to change my mind, yet he was so proud walking down the aisle with me. Mum had spent the previous evening pressing my dad's only good suit. Mum had been worried that she couldn't wear fashionable shoes, her ulcerated legs were heavily bandaged. I still look at my wedding photographs knowing that I wouldn't change anything; I had the most loving parents anyone could wish for. I also loved John's mum, she was a caring, gentle but hardworking woman. His dad rarely spoke to me, but since he has passed to the higher side of life he has communicated a number of times. It is never too late to make amends! My journey has been a contrast of extreme sorrow when we lost our son and also absolute bliss at the pleasure of three living sons, delightful daughters in law, and the most wonderful grand children. I have been blessed with a wonderful family and an abundance of friends.

What more could anyone ask for?

Chapter
3

Up To Date

Thirty years later I find myself packing for another tour of Ireland; three weeks moving from one hotel to another! This is my third visit this year, yet each trip is as refreshing and as rewarding as any other. It has always been a favourite destination. The people are friendly and welcoming and each experience is unique. This particular trip is one I thought I might never complete, as we come towards the end of 2006 the year ends on a high after it began with news that shattered both me and all my family. I had started to feel extremely tired, I was in more pain than usual, and eventually after numerous trips to the specialist I was diagnosed with cancer of the kidney. I was admitted to the Glan Clwyd hospital in North Wales where I had to undertake a number of minor operations before they proceeded to remove the offending kidney. It was a worrying and uncertain time for all of us, but with the support of my loving family I made a full recovery. The operation was a complete success, and a few weeks later I received the news we had all been waiting for - I was given the all clear by the doctors. I really had been given ***a little more time!***

My priority was to complete my second manuscript and fulfil various obligations. I felt pressurised to rest, but I knew the best medicine for me was to continue with my work. The experience had tested me in a way I wasn't prepared for; I have battled illness most of my life, but this time I was both angry and frightened. I questioned why Spirit had brought me this far with my work only to undergo further suffering. It wasn't the fear of dying or returning to Spirit, but being regretful of all the time I could have given to my family. I felt I had failed them as I had devoted the best part of my life to Spirit. On the night before I was due to go into hospital I lay awake for hours in my bed, I couldn't get past an overwhelming feeling of being alone. I was very aware that this may be the last time I would see the familiar surroundings of my home and feel the comfort of my beloved John by my side.

I reminded myself that every day I reassure people that despite their pain, they are never alone, Spirit surrounds them. I am only human after all and I asked Spirit for strength; the following morning I woke feeling an inner calm, aware that my life was in God's hands. By placing my trust in Spirit I was to learn that this difficult time increased my awareness. As I lay in hospital I could feel the love and support of my fellow Spiritualists as they sent healing thoughts and prayers.

At one particular point, I saw a very special friend who had been sending me intense healing, standing at the foot of my bed. The intensity of the energy was so remarkable I was able to see his physical form despite the fact he was alive and well living some fifty or so miles from the hospital. The power of love should never be underestimated, neither should the wonder of Spirit be forgotten, for it is at the most difficult times in our lives that Spirit draw ever closer.

With a fresh purpose and new found energy I threw myself back into my work. This time, I intended to keep my family close and not neglect their needs. I remembered the support and love they had all given during my illness, and straight away we set about arranging a party to celebrate our fiftieth wedding anniversary. It was over six months away but I knew it was going to be a special occasion.

One of the most enjoyable aspects of my work is the variety of tasks; each day is different. Medium-ship is a very responsible role but it is also very rewarding. For many years I served as President of Rhyl Spiritualist National Union Church, but sadly had to relinquish my position when I was diagnosed with cancer. The church played a very large part of my life and it was very difficult to walk away. Some of my most enjoyable responsibilities were to conduct blessing ceremonies (weddings) and naming ceremonies (christenings). These were very joyous events, playing a part in people's important occasions, and I made many lifelong friends. I also conducted funerals and felt honoured that families turned to our church in their time of need. We held many fund raising events to raise money to renovate the church and the congregation were always willing to help in arranging events for charity. It was a full time position in itself, and somehow I also had to arrange all my other commitments.

I tour regularly around the country and visit Ireland and the Channel Islands on a regular basis. As a developing medium, I started working in small churches conducting divine services then as I grew in experience I would work in theatres and large halls giving public demonstrations. I found private sittings rewarding but also physically exhausting; sometimes I would use more energy on a one to one sitting than I would demonstrating to a large audience. At times I would be called out to assist people in their homes when they had been troubled with unexplained disturbances. Rescue work is when we aim to assist those spirits who have for some reason remained earthbound. Each day presents new challenges - no two days are the same. By combining all aspects of my work I never ceased to be enthralled by all the new experiences.

Many mediums are also blessed with healing abilities. Today the training is very rigorous, and it can take many years to reach the desired level. Spiritual surgeons are very rare but I was fortunate to be helped by a gentleman who visited my local area. A demanding schedule in the early months of 2005 had left me feeling both physically and mentally drained. I appeared to be susceptible to all manner of viruses, no sooner had I recovered from one illness, I became vulnerable to another. A dose of influenza followed in quick succession with impetigo, and a chest infection had forced me to reschedule some appointments. Eager as ever to return to work, I had assumed subsequent aches and pains could be easily explained by the simple fact that I had allowed too little time to recuperate. By the end of April, I was suffering from major discomfort. My body ached constantly as though I were consumed by rheumatism, the occasional headache had also escalated into a constant onslaught of blinding migraine. I hadn't realised I had been holding my head to one side for quite some time until one evening in early May 2005; I was relaxing at home when it became apparent that I was unable to move my neck and shoulders. Excruciating pain seared through my limbs, I could no longer tolerate the pain.

I had heard that a reputable healer was visiting the area. Ray Brown is a trance medium, with the assistance of Paul of Tarsus, his remarkable Spirit guide, Ray and his wife Jillian are renowned to have brought considerable relief to thousands of sufferers. I knew I couldn't miss the opportunity of seeing Ray work and inwardly prayed that I might be fortunate enough to secure an appointment with him. If only it was that simple! Complications arose when it appeared I would be unable to travel. Doubled up in agony, the simple task of getting into the car was a nightmare. Eventually with the help of one of my dearest friends, Margaret Stirling, we arrived at the demonstration, after Margaret had successfully avoided all unnecessary bumps and potholes.

Throughout the demonstration I was wriggling in my seat unable to get comfortable; unfortunately there were too many in attendance and I was unable to be seen by Ray Brown. Jillian had noticed my predicament and suggested that if I could attend the following day's healing clinic she would arrange for me to be treated. My first recollection was seeing an intense healing energy. I witnessed Ray's Spirit guide as the treatment commenced. I considered this to be quite a privilege, and from that moment on I felt totally relaxed. Every aspect of the treatment was highly professional. I soon discovered that a number of discs in my back were out of alignment, yet as the healing progressed it became easier to move my neck and shoulders. I remained uncomfortable and very sore but was advised that a follow up treatment would take place in my sleep state two or three days later. I was given some herbal cream to aid the nerve ends, and returned home much brighter than I had left.

My main concern at the time was that I was due to hold a very special demonstration the following evening; it had been arranged quite some time back on behalf of a charitable cause. The next morning I awoke feeling refreshed and uplifted; Paul of Tarsus and his amazing Spirit doctors had enabled me to fulfil my obligation. A few nights later I became aware of a bright light circling my bedroom. I could see myself on a bed and there was an empty bed across from me. I heard a voice say *'We are ready for you now'*, I was convinced I was about to pass to Spirit. Waking up that following morning I was amused to discover how the most mundane aspects of life could appear so invigorating. I was pain free and able to move with ease for the first time in a very long time, thanks entirely to the dedication of a Spiritual surgeon and his wonderful team.

Chapter
4

Going Public

Media attention isn't necessarily as glamorous as it may appear. The pressures can be immense, and the travelling and waiting around is quite draining, but I have always enjoyed the challenge. There is no getting away from the fact that I can reach more people with one television show than I can by spending months touring around the country. In particular I enjoy radio shows; to connect successfully with Spirit you need to link with the sitter's voice, so radio is an excellent way of connecting to the sitter as there are no outside influences. Yet the atmosphere of a public demonstration cannot be beaten. Being able to meet new people and being a part of their experience of connecting with their loved ones is acutely rewarding.

My first stage appearance was quite daunting, it came about at a time when I least expected. I was working in Belfast and the best venue in town had an opening to fill; it was friends who suggested that I take the plunge. Without their encouragement I don't believe I would have had the confidence to go ahead. I was terrified sitting backstage, I kept looking at the clock, counting the minutes, but the moment I walked on that stage Spirit took control and the evening was a huge success. The energy in the hall was a new experience for me, and decades later the wonder has never ceased to amaze me. When I walk on stage I have no idea what will transpire, no Medium can conjure up Spirit, the connection occurs between the love from those here on earth and the bond that unites them with their loved ones in Spirit. Spirit choose to come and provide evidence of their survival, not merely to give comfort to those they left behind but also because they are certain that when we are made aware that we are more than flesh and blood our existence here on earth takes on a whole new dimension. During one particular demonstration, I heard the audience gasp, and my initial reaction was that something embarrassing must have occurred. I checked that my dignity was still intact and I was relieved to see two white butterflies circling around my head. No sooner had I spotted them than they disappeared.

I consider it important to have humour in my work - there is no better medicine than laughter. Many of the people who attend my demonstrations are grieving, so getting the right balance of sincerity and humour is vitally important. I once tripped up as I was crossing the stage and swore before realising I had hundreds of eyes focused on me; I was mortified but fortunately the audience accepted I was human and the sound of laughter filled the hall.

During one demonstration I had the overwhelming energy of an old man with me, who said he was looking for the other room. Immediately I thought he meant the toilets; he said he was looking for his machinery and his projector. He was annoyed that there were so many people in his theatre, and was concerned that they had hidden his projector. It appears he was the gentleman who used to be the theatre projectionist, and on speaking with staff the details emerged of his passion for his work. I felt it was my duty to help him over to the other side but he was adamant that he was staying at his beloved theatre. As far as I am aware his Spirit remains at the theatre.

During one tour my husband John and I were invited to a wedding We arrived at the venue the night before and arranged to meet the family at a pub for a meal. I assure you I remained on the orange juice. (As much as I like the odd tipple or two, when I am away working I abstain from too much alcohol so that I can be at my best to work. I simply make up for it when I get home and have a sherry in the comfort of my own front room.) A gentleman came and stood in front of me; he looked me in the eyes and said he was Charles Henry Ainsworth. I joked and replied, *'Yes, and I am Margaret Hurdman'*. I asked my husband if he knew the gentleman, but he had no idea who he was, I then asked the whole family, each time their reaction was the same. His name was not familiar to anyone. Next morning we dressed up in our finery and set off for the church. I don't balance that well on high heels but I managed to stand up straight until I arrived at the churchyard. I embarrassed myself as I tripped and stubbed my toe on a gravestone, and as I did so, I heard laughter. Looking at the tombstone I was surprised to see the inscription read the name of Charles Henry Ainsworth. It seemed we had had an additional guest at the party. I certainly hope he enjoyed the celebrations as much as I did.

Since working under the spotlight I have had to grow a thicker skin It is so easy to be hurt and misunderstood, so I have learnt to be on my guard against those who take what I say and do out of context. During one particular radio interview I was asked why I didn't know the contact's name. I explained sometimes it is not necessary to provide the name as the details of their personality can prove more evidential. Regardless of my response, the questioner was adamant that I was avoiding the issue; but the reality is, we don't have a say in what Spirit think is appropriate. One communicator may give detailed evidence such as names and dates, another may give a description of their appearance. Everything depends on the personality of the communicator; some come through fast and vibrant, others maybe slow and difficult to communicate with but their personalities are proof in itself that they have survived in Spirit. A public interview, whether it be on the television or radio, is controlled by the person conducting the interview. If they are fair and open minded they treat you fairly; if they have pre-conceived ideas of their own, they have no intention of allowing you to be perceived any other way. Despite the pressures, I could never give up my work. I enjoy the theatre experiences and have many wonderful memories that help me to remain positive at all times.

On my travels I have collected some wonderful memories and they have not always occurred at the actual event I was travelling to. Sometimes the journey itself has been an experience. I was on my way to Jersey to do a tour of demonstrations, and whilst waiting in the departure lounge at Manchester airport I was drawn to a lady waiting for the same flight. I immediately visualised a gentleman with her and realised he had not been in Spirit very long. I instantly became aware that he was her husband; he spoke of children and confided that his wife was emotionally raw as he had only passed over six weeks before. He said she was very frightened and tearful and asked me to keep an eye on her. She had been staying with family but now needed to go home and locate some missing documents. He told me she would find the document in a tin box with an elastic band around it, which was to be found in the garage right next to the pickled onions.

I had no idea how I was going to start up a conversation. I had a packet of sweets in my bag so I reached over and offered her one, then I mentioned that she looked very tired and she confirmed that she was in fact exhausted following the recent death of her husband. I was never going to get a better opportunity than that! So I explained that I had no wish to offend her but I understood she was looking for an important document. She questioned my ability to know such matters; I explained further that I had no wish to invade her privacy but I had been given the information. She looked at me and I saw instant recognition on her face. She acknowledged she had seen an article in her local paper and asked if I was that same person she had read about. At this point she started to ask questions, if I could tell her that her husband was all right, whether he was lonely. I replied that he was fine and that he had met two golfing buddies. I told her where to find the document, and she found it amusing that he had placed such a valuable document beside his prized onions. She commented that she had never been so pleased that a flight had been delayed, we exchanged details and she confirmed that she would let me know if she successfully located the papers.

On the second night of the tour a letter had been left at the theatre for me; the lady had found the document in the exact place I described, she had told her sister what had occurred and they had both attended the previous night's show. How can I not love the work I do? Whilst the lady had to grieve for her personal loss she was now aware the man she had spent her entire life with was still close and she knew she would never feel quite so lonely again.

Not all messages are quite so straightforward. During one demonstration I came across a gentleman who was very obnoxious. I didn't want to go to him but Spirit had other plans. The gentleman refused to accept everything I said to him. One of the details I gave him was that Spirit was telling me that he had lost part of one of his fingers. He still refused to accept any part of the message so I requested that he held his left hand above his head, and when he finally relented it became obvious to all that he had half a finger missing. His response was that it had happened years ago. When I mentioned that it was his father who had given me the message, adding that his father had admitted he had been chopping kindling in the back garden when the accident occurred, the man went pale and said no more. The gentleman still maintained that I had been incorrect, yet two weeks later he contacted me to request a private sitting. He apologised for appearing awkward but had not wanted anyone to know his personal details. By being evasive he drew even more attention to himself. One of the very first things I learnt was to be discreet, and on those occasions when messages are too private for a public demonstration I always requested they met with me later. On this occasion there was nothing to embarrass him and I was surprised why he had chosen to attend in the first place.

When I was invited for an interview for a television programme, my friend Lesley and I felt that because of the distance to London, her old banger might not survive the distance. We hired a small Nissan Micra, and despite its size we whizzed down the motorway in no time at all. It was a long way to go for an interview but we went armed with sandwiches, drinks and goodies to save us money. Thanks to Lesley's knowledge of London we made the journey in good time. When we arrived we immediately went in search of a place for me to change in to my finery. Fortunately there was a local pub near the studios, so we ordered a meal and they must have thought we had come on our holidays as we were laden with bags. The old bird scrubbed up well in the pub's toilets and we proceeded to the interview.

The moment I went through the door I was aware that my high guide was with me and his thoughts were was that this was not for me. I found the interviewer full of her own importance, so I thanked her for her time and explained that I didn't want to waste any more of her time. She looked at me gob smacked and asked if I knew what I was turning my nose up at. She said it would make me famous; my instinct was that it would be more infamous than famous and would bring Spirit into disrepute. They didn't want medium-ship they wanted sensationalism, fiction not fact, and that was the end of the interview. It wasn't a totally wasted journey - we had a delicious bag of chips on the way home! On the first toilet stop I changed back into my comfortable clothes, and we spent most of the journey listening to a pyschic giving spot readings on the radio. It was abysmal but it ended our day on a high as we couldn't stop laughing for the rest of the journey home.

Another time we stretched our limits was when I was invited to work in a London church. I have always been a bit of a scatterbrain and could get lost down a one way street. My friend Lesley said we would give it a go but couldn't promise the car would get us there. Imagine the scenario, Lesley and I thumbing a lift on the motorway, Lesley is thirty years younger than me and might well have been offered a lift, but yours truly would probably still be walking down the hard shoulder! We took the chance as it was too late to hire a car, and went prepared for all eventualities. We arrived in good time, found the church and decided to kill a few hours. It was obvious Lesley knew where she was going, she had lived in the city for many years and took me on a tour of London. I wanted to see where the queen lived, and we made our way to Buckingham Palace.

As we drove down The Mall we were promptly pulled over. Imagine the poor policeman's face when he discovered why we had come to London, we couldn't have looked more suspicious if we had tried! It soon became obvious that he was quite interested in what we did and had decided we were above board, but not before he and his partner made a thorough search of the car. We had Guernsey number plates and they had difficulty finding proof of ownership. Eventually, we were given the all clear; a simple church service involved us being checked by the anti-terrorist branch. It all added to the fun of the day. A quick visit to the Spiritualist Association of Great Britain and it was time to make our way back to the church.

I have learnt that nothing should surprise me. It is experiences such as these that have enabled me to keep my sense of humour intact - without it sometimes I wonder if I could have coped. Spirit give you only what you can handle, and I am grateful for all the magical moments that have come my way as I attempt to continue my work.

Two Orbs over an unaware audience during a show in Cork R.O.I - 2006

I don't have a special effects team - just the spirit for my light show!

Spiritual energy manifested in a shower of Orbs - Burnavon N.I. - 2006

*No, I am not juggling!
- a large Orb whilst demonstrating in Caernarfon, N.Wales 2005*

Myserious Orbs, light, and shadows - electrifying energy in the theatre - Burnavon 2006

Not a great quality picture, yet it looks like I am welcoming this Orb to the demonstration - Jersey

Ready for my stage call!

One of my many radio phone-ins which I enjoy so much.

Chapter
5

Guidance from Abe

I could never have imagined how important a part of my life Abe would become. That energy force I encountered during my first visits to the Spirit world eventually came known to me as my principle guide and Inspirer. In times of uncertainty and confusion, I have often been given guidance from Abe in the form of inspirational writing and poetry. On many occasions when it has been difficult to express the way I feel, or when people have shown difficulty in coming to terms with their loss, Abe has stepped forward and provided a more enlightened understanding.

Abe gave me this verse whilst trying to re-assure a sitter of their need to be patient.

The River

The river starts in a very small way
As on its journey it flows, it gathers strength.
It twists and turns over rocks making new ground
Finally at the source of the river it is a torrent
Then eventually it reaches its goal the sea.
Like as to our first awareness of our faith
It is slow it gathers strength
As each twist and turn of life we progress
We overcome the rocks and rough patches of our days
At the end of the journey we will be strong
Strong in the certain wisdom everything that is planned for us
Is planned from the start
The start of our earthly life until we reach our end.

This verse was given during a sitting with a gentleman whose best friend had drowned. He couldn't understand the futility of his friend's loss; as fishermen they were wise to the nature of the sea, and his friend had been a particularly strong swimmer.

Hope

The man who sails the sea, he puts his trust in the weather
The compass, map and navigator, each plays its own part.
He protects himself from danger
He has a life jacket
To save himself should the storm wash him overboard,
This is not a lack of trust, this is protection.

When a man thinks about his beliefs
He questions past influences;
Influences that have led him on his journey,
How he has weathered the storm,
How he has been guided on his course.
The map he has is the map of life that has been planned for him
He also has his own navigator, his guide.
His conviction of good
His conviction of life after death
This is his anchor against doubts and fears, his course is clear
No storm will make him falter
This man protects himself from all harm,
This is the protection of true spirit.

When man's sailing days are over
He has weathered all life's storms.
The time is right to move to safe harbour
Then he hands himself to his maker,
At rest in God's loving care, to sail the seas of time
At peace with the world
Rough seas no more.

I had been told of a local crowd of youths who had beaten a cat to death. The cruelty had played on my mind for many days when this was given to me.

Animals

The animals of this life are blessed
No angry words spoken to each other
No brutality inflicted, only nature's plan.
They do not know and understand the evil in many men's minds
They do not covet what others have
Most animals only ask for love of man
An animal mainly kills to eat
This we understand.

Man will kill for lust and fun,
Stupid man does he know or understand
The wrong he has done?
In this world of hate and greed
Why must man hurt other beings so?
Every living being in this life
Has its purpose on this earth's plan.
Again I say why must man hurt others so?
In the better world to come when animal and man meet again
Man has many deeds and words to explain.

I became very fond of a neighbour's child who often came to sit with me. At times she would make comments that were surprising for such a young child. She told me that she was never going to be a big lady as she was going to live with Jesus; at the time I assumed it was her family's strong Catholic influence. Her family moved house but she was tragically killed before she started school. Fifteen years later I visited the area her family had moved to and decided to put flowers on her grave. I had difficulty locating the gravestone and eventually asked directions from the grounds man. As he pointed me in the right direction, a strong light hit the brow of the hill highlighting the position of the stone; as I drew closer I heard her say *"Hello Auntie Maggot",* the affectionate name by which she used to call me.

Julia

The little ray of sunshine beaming from heaven above
Nestled on our child at play on an ordinary summers day
The light shone on her golden curls
Her innocence radiates from within
She asks no favours, no rich rewards
She in her innocence knew no greed or strife
This was the purpose of her short earthly life

She was loaned from God above,
She came to show us perfect love
The summer in her smile radiates from within
She only came for a little while to share her light
Not long after that summer's day she went on her way
She returned to the perfect life, we miss her so.
Why did she have to go?

We ask our God above, loved her so
Again we ask 'why did she have to go?'
The answer came to our earnest plea:
She will never feel pain,
This child of love, child of God, will live again
When the time is right, together we will be again

Abe gave me the following words during a sitting with a gentleman who was struggling with the loss of his wife. They had been blessed with a close loving relationship, and he had become so despondent when he was unable to personally communicate with her following her passing.

With You

When you call for me I am there;
I hear you cry at night
I sense your despair.
Do not think because you cannot see me, I am not there.
I am there when the breeze ruffles your hair,
When the smell of a familiar perfume is in the air,
Cry not my love I am never far away.
Who did you think it was when the door opened silently?
That was me.

I kiss your cheek when you are asleep,
When a memory stirs in your mind,
A smile drifts across your face,
The memory of a past embrace; I am with you.
The days are long for you I know,
There is still much for you to do on earth below.
Please, my dear, live your life to the full,
There are undone things that have to be done.

I promise you when there is nothing you have left to do
Then, my love, I will come for you;
I will await the divine call from above
I will hold your hand to lead you over to the Promised Land.
No more tears, no more pain, reunited we will be again.
Do not fear, you are not alone,
Tomorrow is another day.

I am only a whisper away

I was talking to a man whose wife had suffered absolute agony with cancer of the spine. He was missing her immensely, and whilst he had felt her around him since her passing, he still couldn't come to terms with the fact she had to suffer so much.

Lost

I look into my heart
What do I see?
I see the hurt that is deep within me.
Never to hold you close again
I sit on my own, lonely and sad
Missing you as I do
Our love was honest, good and true.

I find it hard to adjust to being without you,
Knowing I must not think selfishly.
To wish you back to pain
Would be the cruellest thing anyone could do
Forgive me, dear, I cannot do this to you.

For a moment I forget my pain,
Next second it's there again.
Yesterday I moved your books
I'm sure I heard you say
Cry not dear, tomorrow is another day.
I feel your gentle touch upon my
neck, a whispered caress.

I know now, I am glad to say
You have not gone completely away
Your spirit remains, your love lives on around me every day
I will wait my dear for a better time,
Then you and I will go
To that wonderful place called heaven above.
No more tears
No more pain
You and I will be reunited again.

A lady came to visit me after years of wanting to have a baby; eventually she became pregnant but suffered with a severe chest infection whilst carrying the child, and the child was born with Down's syndrome. Not long after the child's birth her husband passed away leaving her alone to raise the child.

Loan

When you smile at me what do you see?
Do you see my tired wrinkled face?
Or my unspoken embrace?
Can you see the love I give to you?
This is the inner me
To laugh and smile when days chores are to be done.
I wash and feed, clean put you right
To start the day my son

I look at you and inwardly say, why must it be so?
You never know the joys of play,
Never to know the life that others have every day.
I must not complain, I have you on loan today,
Every day a special day:
I hope and pray, tomorrow will be another day

You do not see the unshed tears, the hurt I feel
When a stranger looks at you, then looks again
Sighs and says 'poor boy', why must it be so?
Only God knows; never mind, dear son
God and your mother love you so.

The love that radiates from your smile
Makes all the hurt worthwhile;
The gentleness as you stroke your face
This is your inner grace.
I thank my God for loaning you to me
The love we share is very rare;
I have you and you have me.

I was thinking of a dear friend and blaming myself for not seeing her before she passed. Remembering good times together, I regretted losing touch and not saying goodbye and so wished I could turn back time.

Smile For Me

Do not blame yourself my friend,
Do not cry,
There is a time for everyone to die.
Some souls live a long time on earth's realms
This for me was not to be
Please my friend do not be sad
Think of laughter shared.
No one can take this from you and me
Again I say to you, what is to be will be.

When you talk of me
Do not talk with a solemn air;
This should not be.
Remember my friend, I am me,
You cannot see me, I am there;
You cannot touch me, I am there;
My friend, I share your joy of fun shared together,
Of days gone by.
You must go on, laugh and laugh again,
Remember me with fun;
Remember me with a smile.
Cry no more.
We did not have time to say goodbye,
Many years from now
When you came my way
You and I will be able to say
God works in a mysterious way.

So many people have asked me what is the point of life, with all the hardship, struggle and pain that so many have to bear. I was mulling over a lady's comments when Abe provided me with the following insight.

The Sand of Time

Every grain of sand has a purpose
Every being is part of a divine plan.
Think not only of wealth,
Even poverty has a plan.
When we see what others have
We know for sure that material wealth hath no score.
We thank our God and say
Blessed I am for I have my God at my side.
Poor lonely man, who does not know that he is part of life's plan
He has no hope, he has no joy,
Bitterness and greed, no faith hath he.
His is the loss of humanity
The light that could be his has yet to learn to shine.

As his journey onward goes, what will he learn?
Will he hold in his palm the knowledge of eternal love?
If this is so, he will know what life is about
We will not pity him so, for he will
know onward, onward to go.

The blessed man who knows for sure, the way he travels is true
He has the pure of heart and deed in all that he can do.
He gives the best of all he has, he knows no greed,
This man is truly a blessed man, he is part of the heavenly plan.
Lucky God fearing spirit man, this is the part of the eternal plan
As the sand of time sifts through the breeze
Our grain of sand, our maker knows its resting place
Every grain is part of the completed plan.

On another occasion when people asked me about the purpose of life, I was given the following words comparing man's life to that of a tree.

The Tree

The tree is like a man's life,
His roots are deep, they hold secure,
From the roots grows the trunk,
From the trunk follow the branches,
The leaves and the blossoms.
As earthly life progresses
So man grows a stature,
He then puts out branches
These are likened to arms,
To embrace the world
These are the fruits of spiritual life.
When man's life is finished
He is called to a higher place.
The flowers and leaves fall and wither.
The branches break.
The trunk needs no substance.
Very often the roots remain; they are deep,
This is like man's earthly life
He leaves his deep thoughts behind.
Memories, they last long after man has passed
To a higher life.

A lady knocked on my door; she had come straight from the cemetery where she had buried her daughter. As they laid the child to rest a beautiful rainbow formed directly above. She was keen to find out if the rainbow held any significance.

Rainbow

The rainbow of a child's smile is plain for all to see.
When my child smiles at me
I forget the naughty things she did,
I know all is well for a while.
I laugh at her cheeky smile,
Her innocence radiates, her love surrounds all.
Please is the password to success
No one can resist her meekness
Sunshine radiates from within
Her smile would win anyone's heart
The rainbow of her love sets her apart.

A gentleman asked me if when he passed over, would he be judged by God. It is our belief that we are judged by ourselves, as when we pass we are able to see how we lived our life.

Wings of time

Flow gently on wings of time,
Flow gently child of God, child of light.
The world and man has much to learn,
Each soul knows the mistakes he left behind.
Empty your mind of grief, hate, strife, vanity
Leave all behind.

I have a plan to make the earth a better place.
If man on earth would listen, with an open mind, open heart
Then love, poor, holy love would preside.
Man will only hear if he wishes to hear,
He will only see what he wishes to see,
Be still and listen, true this I tell you.

A man walks tall head held high,
Shoulders back, his aim is clear.
Doubt not the wisdom of this man;
He is sincere, this man trusts his God.
He acts on what he thinks is right,
He tries to help fellow man;
Trust the good in the inner man,
Trust the better part of man within

Sad man that walks with no purpose to his life, he has far to go.
He doubts what God has said, he doubts the good in man.
This I tell you; so
Be like the man who walks tall and sure.
Your purpose in life is clear, I am near I will never leave you,
I will be at your side, trust in me child.
I am the part of the eternal plan, your friend and guide.

One of my sitters came to me full of remorse, hurt and sorrow, he felt so alone and totally lost. Without his wife, life had lost all meaning and purpose.

Alone

The time that I have dreaded has come my way,
With fear for the future my heart cries out in pain.
My love, do not leave me to face the world alone,
I am afraid in many ways.
The days are long, the loneliness tears me apart.
Why must there be for me another day?

Please give me the strength to face the oncoming day.
If I could turn back time I would hold you close,
I would never let you go, I loved you so.
Forgive me love, I am a selfish soul,
I should not wish you back to pain.

I feel your presence everywhere, I hear you sigh.
Why did you have to go and leave me alone?
I pray to God above please take me to my love,
In my despair on bended knees, I asked for help from God above
The words he said I felt in my heart.

Do not weep, your love is in a better place.
She has no more pain, do not wish her back again,
In the realms of light she lives again.
When the time is right for you to come
You will join your love, and together you will both live again.
Be assured have faith, have trust
you will be together again.

This next verse was given to me during a sitting with a pompous man who was planning to build a memorial in honour of his friend's memory. All around him, family and friends were struggling, but at the time he thought it was apt to create a monument rather than help those in real need. Learning humility was a valuable lesson to him.

Life

If you ever have wondered why,
Why man is born to die
This my friend I tell you,
There is a plan for everyone in this life.
If you are born with gifts of material wealth
Think not that only you are blessed;
You my friend have the greater test.
The testing time of your wealth has to come;
Ask for wisdom to see that material wealth
Is not all that you think it to be,
Ask for compassion, eyes to see the need of fellow man
Give to others who cannot give to you.

The man who has nothing
Came into this world, no rich silks adorned his skin.
This man that has no material wealth
Can give freely of what he has;
This may be an understanding heart;
It may be love and compassion for others.
These for sure are the greater gifts
That set men apart.
When the end of man's life has come
The counting time is due;
The man who has given the best he can
Is the man who loves his fellow man.
His spirit sets him apart, this part of God within
Pure loving soul of the heart,
Born with nothing, has fulfilled his life's span,
Returns to his maker; the lesson of life that he had to learn is done
This is man of God within.

A gentleman came for a sitting, he was tired and had been ill for some time, and he questioned his need to remain in this world. The following helped him to realise that every part of his life had a plan, that when, and only when, it was time for him to return would he return to spirit.

A Time

There is a time for being born
A time for dying.
It is the time in between that decides
The purpose of the life to follow;
If a man can say at the end of the day
I have done my best in every way.
Honesty must be his aim
To look and see his fellow man, and feel no shame.
Goodness and love must be in his heart,
The God within keeps this man from mortal sin
When this soul is on his journey to the other side
All will know God to be his guide.

The man that is born with hate for fellow man
Has no hope in the eternal plan.
Poor man he has no faith, he has no joy,
On his journey he doth go.
He sows the seeds of discontent, a word cruelly said
This can break some poor man's heart.
We can hope he sees the error of his ways
When onward he goes,
He will say 'God forgive me and my sinful ways'
Forgive me God, he prays.

Chapter
6

Development

There is without doubt much change in the public's perception of the work we do as mediums. When I first started to develop my abilities, most mediums were viewed as being at the worst fraudulent, at the best misguided. Over the last thirty years the general opinion has changed; people now tend to be more open minded and intrigued. As a fledgling medium my work was often looked at with contempt by those who had not been touched with a personal experience; today most people I come across are curious and fascinated. I honestly believe this is a sign of the times and I also believe the interest will continue to grow until our work becomes a normal and accepted aspect of the human existence. When the work we do is abused and misunderstood, it frustrates and angers me to the very core. To see how these changes have transformed in my lifetime has been one of my most rewarding experiences. Spiritualism has indeed evolved in a way I never expected to see; from those first reported incidences in Hydesville, USA many individuals have dedicated their lives definitively proclaiming the revelation of spirit communication.

During 160 years of the spiritualist movement there have been many changes; the old myths that had been perpetuated have in today's society finally been laid to rest. No longer are we associated with the dark side of life. Mediums can at last be seen for the reality of the work they achieve. Superstition and hocus pocus is now a thing of the past, we are now in a position to make a real difference to those lives we touch. The possibilities are an inspiration, the future is bright.

I have put together a brief synopsis of those first pioneering mediums and proponents of Spiritualism without whom my work would have been made considerably more difficult. This information is presented in Appendix I, "Out of the Dark Ages".

Mediumship

Medium-ship is the ability to see things beyond what is normally accepted. The art of clairvoyance is one of the most natural senses; everyone has the ability to communicate with Spirit, but very few people are aware of this faculty. The majority of people will live their lives unaware of one of their most fascinating senses. Many people are born spiritually aware, others like myself discover the ability at some later stage in life.

There are three main senses; clairvoyance is the ability to see Spirit but is used as the general term for having the ability to communicate. Clairaudience is the ability to hear Spirit and clairsentience is the ability to sense Spirit. Development can be quite complex which is why many people give up at the first hurdle. It is certainly not the easiest ability to develop, but it is surely one of the most rewarding. It takes much dedication, time and effort to master; you need discipline to maintain growth and advancement. The work of a medium is to prove the survival of Spirit; most mediums aspire to give meaningful evidential messages, to be able to prove without any doubt that a sitter's loved one has survived in the Spirit world. Every medium works differently, but all mediums connect with a higher energy by raising their vibration, in turn Spirit lower their vibration and the medium is then able to be used as a channel for Spirit to communicate. Everyone has a primary guide, some people might refer to them as being their guardian angel. This guide is there from a person's conception to the time they return to Spirit. A medium learns to communicate with their guide, they learn to trust instinctively what their guide communicates to them. As a medium develops they will encounter numerous different guides who all provide different qualities, depending on the need at the time. The closer the medium becomes to their guides, the stronger the communication channel will become. In order to strengthen this link the medium learns to sit in the energy.

Prepare yourself to sit in the energy by finding somewhere comfortable to sit. Ideally you need a straight back chair, and you need to sit upright with your feet firmly on the floor. Place your hands, palms down on your knees, take a deep breath, relax and close your eyes. There is nothing unnatural or frightening to fear, but just like on the earth not everyone is sweetness and light, there are those in Spirit who are not necessarily good natured. By surrounding yourself in love and light the natural law is that only those of love and light will be able to draw close to you. To do this simply imagine a powerful light surrounding your body enveloping you like a cloak. Draw it around you as if it were a warm comforting coat on a cold wintry night. Feel the protection and the warmth it provides as the light covers every inch of your body. I always say a little prayer and ask that as I step forward into the light only those of light and love be allowed to draw close to me. It is now time to relax your breathing; breathe slowly and deeply, feel your body starting to relax. Leave behind the worries of the day; this is your time to feel at ease with yourself.

Now it is time to learn to open your energy centres and raise your vibration. We have seven energy centres in the body, these are otherwise known as chakras. Attending a development circle will teach you how to locate each centre and to visualise the opening of each chakra. *See chart opposite to learn the location and colour of each chakra.*

A common exercise to open the chakra is to imagine placing a closed rosebud or door at the location of each chakra. Gradually imagine the rosebud or door starting to open, take a deep breath and imagine that wonderful light being drawn into your body to the point where the chakra is placed.

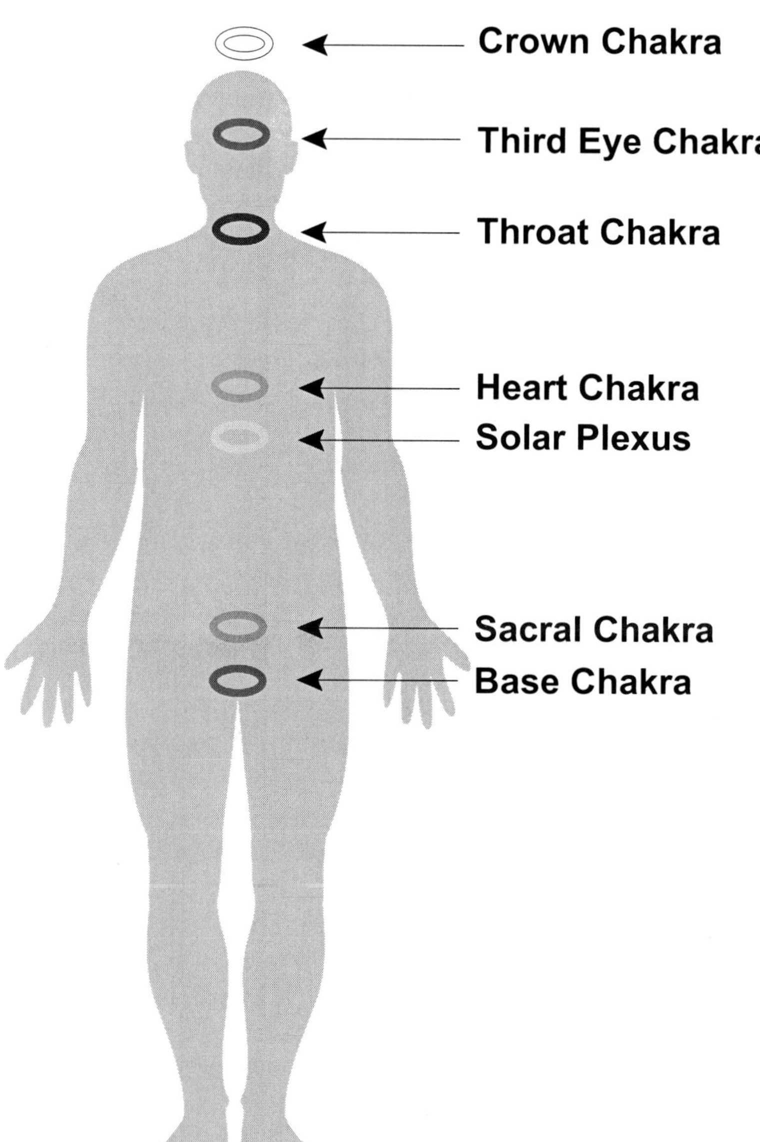

The Seven Chakras

The visualisation will help to open the energy centre. Initially you start at the top of the head, then move down to the base of the spine; breathing deeply visualise the white light drawing through your body. Once you have opened the chakra situated at the base of the spine, visualise a red light drawing up through the earth; this is what we call grounding ourselves. As the red light combines with the white light, imagine the two energies combining in your solar plexus area. Once all seven chakras have been opened you are open to Spirit and the learning begins.

Don't expect to automatically be all seeing and hearing. The process is gradual. Many people are under the illusion that when a medium hears Spirit they hear with their ears, the reality is that a medium hears with the mind. It is a thought placed in the medium's mind, and as you develop you will hear a common phrase, *"first thought is Spirit, second thought is your own"*. Always remember when you have opened to Spirit, it will be the first thought that you have that is being provided by Spirit. If you have to think long and hard it is probably your own thoughts. By the same token, when a clairvoyant sees, they see an image in what we call our third eye, it is the point where the chakra is located on our forehead. Whenever I work, my forehead becomes increasingly red in colour. This does not necessarily happen to everyone who is clairvoyant.

Meditation

Raising your energy requires you to be relaxed and comfortable. Meditation is an excellent way to relax both your mind and body. I find it is much easier to relax with beautiful music - the type of music that enables you to escape and imagine being in calm surroundings. With a clear mind you are much more open to Spirit, so it is important to learn how to meditate and leave your earthly cares behind, if only temporarily.

Astral Travel

It is not essential to experience astral travel in order to develop your senses. It is however something you might wish to be aware of as you develop. Not everyone has the ability to do it, but most people astral travel whilst they are asleep. Our physical bodies are surrounded by our etheric body; this is the part of us that travels when people have out of body experiences. Our etheric body is attached to our physical body by a silver thread, and only when we pass back to Spirit does that thread break. During normal meditation you do not leave your body. When I was seeking answers about myself I dropped off to sleep asking my guides to show me what was expected of me. I rose from my bed and felt I was in another dimension. Due to my artificial eye I had always lacked personal confidence. I had always felt ugly, even on my wedding day as I stood beside my wonderful husband, I questioned his reason for loving me. As I was suspended in time I could see people of all nationalities, people of all sizes, colour and creed and I was reminded that we are all the same regardless of our physical appearance, and most importantly that everyone, yes, even me, was worthy of love.

Premonitions

Very often Spirit draw close in the early hours of the morning and communicate during the sleep state - but then they don't have to wake up to an alarm and rush out to work! Seriously it is not always welcomed when you wake feeling tired, but I learnt to keep a pen and paper beside my bed to recall every experience. We are all capable of having premonitions. I have had many over the years, sometimes it is overwhelmingly frustrating when you see something but are unable to change the course of events. I once had a premonition about a bus crashing into a bus stop with fatal consequences. Two days later I heard that a bus ploughed into a bus stop when the brakes had failed. I had no way of knowing where or when the incident would take place. It is an aspect of my ability that I have always questioned. If only I could be given just a little bit more information then maybe I could do some good. I have never received a premonition about myself or anyone I personally know, but I can sense when something is about to go wrong. Over thirty years I have had prior knowledge of major catastrophes; it is without a doubt one of the hardest things you have to adapt to.

Many mediums suffer from bad health, and it is important to maintain an optimum level of fitness whenever possible. Some mediums are constantly drained and tired, and there is an extremely high rate of diabetes found in working mediums. Eating a sensible diet, taking exercise and generally taking care of yourself are common sense practices that not all people take heed. I must admit when I was originally informed of the energy loss I didn't pay much attention. Seeing many friends tire, and learning first hand of the exhaustion, I eventually sat up and started listening to the advice given. One of the most important lessons I learnt was remembering to close down after I had finished working. Just as we opened our energy centres, the chakras,, we always have to remember to close down. It only takes a matter of seconds but it can make a world of difference to your energy levels. Otherwise Spirit would be pulling on your energy twenty four hours a day. All you have to do is visualise that door or rosebud closing tightly again. Place it on each of the chakras but now in reverse order. Close down all the centres as you once opened them and you will go a long way in helping yourself to be as fit and energetic as you need to be.

Protection

When people first consider developing clairvoyance one of the most common questions is whether it is safe to do so. There is absolutely nothing to fear, because when we come to the section about protection, we are talking primarily about protecting our energy levels. One point that should also be remembered is that mediums are open to psychic attack mainly from other people who may be jealous of their ability or standing. A simple visualisation once you have opened and closed your chakras will prevent most attacks from occurring. Once I have opened my energy centres I visualise red and gold silks being tied around my waist. I then place a solid steel shield in front of my solar plexus, strong enough to protect my body from any negative energies or influences. I do the same when I close the centres; it is a very simple procedure but extremely effective.

Developing your senses is extremely enlightening and rewarding, there are many aspects to this work and you will be guided in the right direction for you. I have tried to incorporate the many sides of clairvoyance in my work, from being the president of a Spiritual church, to demonstrating in large halls all over the world. One thing for sure you will never be bored, for each day brings with it fresh challenges. I will never stop learning and trust that I will never cease to be amazed at the wonder of Spirit.

Chapter
7

A View of the Paranormal

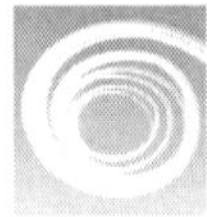

Over the years the paranormal has intrigued and also confused so many, and myths have sprung up out of ignorance. The truth is that Spirit communication is the most natural and fundamental process. The only difference between ourselves and our loved ones in Spirit is that we are Spirit in human form. All of us will leave our bodies at some stage and return from whence we came. Instead of fearing death the truth is that returning to Spirit will be returning to what is familiar to us. We came from Spirit and we will all return. Spirit choose to provide evidence of their survival to ease our journey and life lessons. No one need ever feel alone, for everyone has their own guide, but many are too narrow minded to even think of the possibility. However, times are changing and there is now a wealth of people throughout all cultures who are prepared to seek a greater understanding of themselves.

Ghosts

One of the most common misconceptions is that Spirit and ghosts are one and the same. The truth is that when a house is considered to be haunted it doesn't necessarily mean there are lost spirits roaming the premises. Buildings can retain a residual energy, the energy of an event that once took place within it. Imagine a tape recorder being re-wound and replayed capturing an event that once took place. Sometimes the energy that is created during violent events, for example, can leave a substantial force field and it is this that is considered to be a ghostly apparition, an image of what has gone before.

It is possible that some Spirit for whatever reason can remain earthbound; examples such as the Theatre projectionist that I mentioned earlier in Chapter 4 are tied to a previous existence as they are unable to let go and move forward. Others may pass in difficult circumstances and are unable to come to terms with their situation. I must stress that this is rarer than you would think, and those who wish to be helped to the light can be released quite easily.

Poltergeists

Poltergeists are mainly mischievous spirits and are normally linked with pubescent children. There is considerable fear connected with a poltergeist, but imagine if everyone could see, as many mediums can, the fear would be eliminated, just as you wouldn't be afraid of a naughty child that we can see. The only thing that is truly frightening is fear itself.

Witches

Witches were the old herbalists of yesterday; they made remedies from herbs, and the myths grew from simple superstition. Today many white witches can be found practising quite openly. These people respect and love mother earth and have absolutely no connection with bad energy.

Tools

When Mediums and psychics develop their ability it can be helpful to use various tools such as the following:

- **Tarot Cards**

Tarot cards are used as a focal point and can be very accurate, often depicting past, present and future. A good reader is able to tune into the sitter by focusing on the images on the cards. Other psychics have been known to use crystal balls; again it is just another method for the psychic to tune their energy.

- **Rune Stones**

The Runes originated hundreds of years ago; they are small stones portraying symbols. When thrown against a wall or across a table, according to the way the stones fall, they can provide an answer to a given question.

- **Tea Leaves**

It was quite common for people to get together with a nice cup of tea to debate their future. The tea had to be freshly brewed, and once the tea had been drunk the cup would be turned upside down. How the dregs would fall allowed the reader to interpret the symbols, patterns and shapes of the tea leaves. My Gran was very popular with the neighbours; they would call at her house with a little bag of tea in their hands wrapped up in paper. It was harmless enough, and mainly considered a means of creating companionship and making new friends.

- **Playing Cards**

Ordinary playing cards were also used, much in the same way as the Tarot; the cards were merely used as a focal point.

- **Crystals**

Crystals are formed when water combines with an element under certain conditions of pressure, temperature and energy. When conditions are right, water will cause the element to grow as a crystal. Not only do crystals amplify body energy but thoughts as well. They create power and clarity of thinking. There are many types of crystals, and all are thought to provide different qualities.

- **Pyschometry**

When an item or object is given to the reader to interpret, the emotions of the owner of the article may be sensed. On occasions it is a valuable method to link with the owner. For example, in cases where a crime has been committed, mediums have been able to ascertain valuable information about the owner's life and have been successful in solving a crime or locating missing people.

- **Ribbons**

Ribbons are an addition to psychometry; very often the reader will offer the sitter a choice of ribbons. Frequently, colours were significant and would convey information to the reader. Ribbons were the first tool of medium-ship that I ever used. They were a means of confidence building.

- **Horoscopes and Astrology**

One of the oldest methods of divination and seeking of knowledge is the stars. There are some very accomplished astrologers who with their skill can predict the ways of the planet and how the elements will affect a person on the earth plane. Very often the enquirer will give their birth date and the time they were born. To the skilled astrologer this can mean so much and can help to determine the enquirer's way of life.

- **Palmistry**

To an experienced palmist hands can talk; the lines on our hands are unique, and the palmist can distinguish circumstances of our birth and discern our future.

- **Water Divination/Rods**

Very often, especially in countries with a lack of water, people would use two sticks or metal rods as a means of locating water beneath the ground. The pull of the energy from the ground would literally force the rods to cross where water could be located. This would have the same effect with various different elements such as metals.

Chapter
8

Questions and Answers

I first realised that I could see, hear and communicate with Spirit after my traumatic experiences of visiting the Spirit world. Some people are born spiritually aware whilst others like me, develop later on in life. This can be a hard adjustment to make. Learning to accept and understand a new aspect of yourself can be so daunting. There were so many questions I needed answering, so much I desperately wanted to know and understand. I will never stop learning. Over the years, I have formed opinions of my own and learnt from many sources. I understand the frustrations of an inquisitive mind and have therefore compiled a list of questions that I am asked on a regular basis. This chapter gives a basic understanding and insight into what I have personally come to believe.

Q. What is the difference between a psychic and a medium?

The medium communicates with a higher energy, the evidence given relates to proof of survival. Most mediums have a team of guides who provide different qualities to their medium-ship. Everyone has a primary guide who remains with them from their conception until they return to Spirit. The other guides draw close whenever certain attributes or qualities are needed. A psychic can read a person's aura, they are intuitive and can pick up on earthly situations centred around an individual. Most mediums are also psychic but not all psychics are mediumistic.

Q. How long after someone has passed to Spirit does it take before they can communicate?

Spirit can communicate within seconds of passing, depending on their awareness. Sometimes it may take a matter of weeks, months or even years. There are many factors involved such as the awareness and attitude of both the communicator and the receiver.

Q. I have been married twice, who will I be with?

You will be met by all your loved ones. There is complete unity of mind, no jealousy. Such emotions are earth bound.

Q. Does it matter whether you are buried or cremated?

Once the body has ceased to function the soul leaves and returns to Spirit. The body is simply like an old overcoat that you have since outgrown. You have no purpose for it anymore, therefore how you dispose of a person's physical remains is just a matter of personal choice.

Q. Can Spirit make contact through dreams?

Most definitely. When you are relaxed, Spirit can communicate much more easily. Sleep induces a perfect channel as we have no inhibitions or fears. More often than not, the mind is over active and dreams have no significance. There are times when I have gone to bed not feeling that I have done everything that I should have; inevitably I dream of running and hurrying but getting nowhere, and in my dream I feel frustrated and I wake up feeling very tired. A visit from Spirit is very vivid, and unlike most dreams that are forgotten on wakening, every aspect of the visit will be remembered.

Q. Do ghosts exist?

The pre-conception of a ghost is a haunting figure that roams the earth leaving people frantic with fear. The reality is, it is a rare occasion when a Spirit remains earthbound. The majority of what people regard as ghostly apparitions are simply a residue energy that remains long after they have passed to Spirit. A prime example of this is when you walk into a room, despite not being present when an argument took place, you can feel the tension in the air. Most reputed haunted buildings are sites where extreme behaviour has occurred, such as in the case of the scene of a murder or traumatic accident.

Q. What is a poltergeist?

A poltergeist is the energy of a confused Spirit; it is extremely rare to come across a genuine case. Most incidents are centred around young teenage girls. The energy builds on fear and confusion, more often than not the rogue energy was a young person who had not known love in their earthly life. I was requested to visit the home of a family who had been driven to despair by objects being destructively thrown across the room. After much discussion a member of the family admitted to holding séances in the home, inviting negative energies that manifested and plagued the fourteen year old daughter of the family. On this particular occasion I discovered the energy of a young lad who had passed at the tender age of fourteen; he had felt that he had been denied a chance at life. Only when I was able to explain how he could progress was he able to accept his situation, and I was able to help him pass to the Spirit world with the help of Abe, my primary guide.

Q. How will I know where to go when I die?

I know that on passing over there is always someone to come for you even if you have no loved ones in Spirit. I recall sitting with a friend as she passed to Spirit, the sheer joy she experienced as her dear mother came for her. I felt privileged to have been there, my friend's face was illuminated with happiness.

Q. What is it like to be dead?

Death is completely natural, it is like going to sleep; all pain ceases to exist on the point that the Spirit leaves the body. If you have ever endured real pain or had to sit and watch a loved one suffer, please be assured that all pain and suffering is extinguished. There is a time of adjustment, a time to assess our lives. We are a free Spirit, surrounded by the Spirits of our loved ones, free to progress at our will.

Q. What is hell?

We create our own hell. The majority of people know what is wrong and what is evil. I believe we have to account for our mistakes and wrong doings. Upon reaching the Spirit world, you are soon enlightened to a higher understanding. You are able to analyse your life, you look into your heart and judge yourself. You become aware of your misgivings. I believe very strongly that we judge ourselves, for who knows us better than ourselves. It is the choice of the Spirit; if they are satisfied with what they have learned and accordingly they choose to progress spiritually to higher levels of understanding. I also believe hell is on earth, and we have to live with our own torment. I strongly believe we have to find our own peace of mind. In doing so we have the choice to return to this material world in order to gain further insight and continue to make progress.

Q. Do animals have a soul?

Yes, I do believe they do. They are different to us but they have a greater sense of awareness than we do. I have received considerable proof of survival relating to peoples much loved pets.

Q. Will my family know me?

When you walk on the other side of life you will be welcomed with open arms. They accept you with love, they know your failings, and you have no reason to hide, for there are no secrets. Your soul is unique, so just as you would be recognised by your physical appearance and characteristics on the earth, your soul will be instantly recognisable. It is your soul that truly identifies who you are.

Q. Do you believe there is a God?

Yes, I perceive God as being a loving energy, not dominating, not cruel or judgmental, simply the most powerful and loving energy that exists.

Q. Why does God allow bad things to happen?

I don't believe it is simply a matter that God allows such things to happen. People generally envisage God as being a man who controls the world. The reality is that God is an energy force, whilst he can help, only men can determine their destiny.

Q. Do people who commit suicide get punished?

Absolutely not. Whilst I believe there is an allotted time to pass back to Spirit, a time to be born and a time to die, I strongly believe that those who suffer enough to take their own lives will be comforted and taken care of. It is, however, not an answer to earthly problems, as eventually they will have to return in order to make further Spiritual progress. Suicide in many cases is a cry from the heart for help and understanding, and our God understands each and everyone of us. Probably the learning curve of a suicide has not been fulfilled and I am certain that they will, if they wish, be given the chance to complete their Earth Plan of learning.

Q. My daughter passed as an infant; will she grow up in Spirit?

Yes, your child will grow, but you will instantly recognise her soul. My son passed when he was still a baby, and on my first visit to the Spirit world he was shown to me as being a young boy. Over the years I have been fortunate to see him grow into a man.

Chapter
9

Messages from the Ether

I am often asked what aspects of my work I enjoy the most. Without any hesitation, I can honestly say it is the ability to make a difference, that moment of recognition on a sitter's face when Spirit provides me with evidence that is consistent with the life of a deceased loved one. When Spirit draw close and give me insight into their personality and physical characteristics, it is almost as if I had provided the sitter with a heavy dose of anaesthetic. I can see a look of wonder and relief that has never ceased to amaze me.

At times the interaction with others has been so intense the experience created a unique bond between myself and the sitter, and strong friendships have been formed. One of my most memorable recollections is when I met Margaret Astbury. At the time I was a member of the Lions Club, and I received a phone call from another member of the association, who had rung to see if I would be willing to help a lady who was on holiday staying at a guest house not far from my home. Her husband had just passed away in the local hospital. Despite her obvious pain, I was made to feel very welcome. As we relaxed into each other's company she spoke about herself. In normal circumstances, the less you know about the sitter the easier it is to work. Yet I felt that Margaret needed to talk; her grief was all too raw, her vulnerability struck me to the very core.

It soon became evident that she possessed a most enlightened mind. She spoke on many subjects and then recalled the memory of her first fiancé who never returned from world war two. As she spoke, his Spirit instantly appeared beside her. He told me his name and proudly boasted that he was the love of Margaret's life. He smiled broadly and faded away. In his place stood a man who told me that he was Margaret's first husband, he confirmed his identity and then went on to assure Margaret that he had their son with him. As her son stepped forward I felt the most excruciating pain in my ears; it appeared that he had tragically passed away with an infection of the inner ear and complications caused by a cerebral abscess. Standing alongside Margaret's son stood a little girl; his sister, who had passed back to Spirit during the early stages of pregnancy. It was obvious that at this most difficult time, Margaret's nearest and dearest had drawn close to her, and the strength she obtained from their presence was immense. As her children stepped back, her second husband stepped forward. His body was presently lying in the local undertakers but his Spirit was vibrant as he joked about spoiling the holiday. It is on occasions such as this that I am reminded of the wonder of Spirit. Twelve years later, we remain the closest of friends.

Of course not all the messages are given during private sittings. It would be impossible to honour all the requests that I receive. I tour extensively and some of the most remarkable evidence has been provided at public demonstrations. I was working in Ireland presenting an evening of clairvoyance, when halfway through the evening I was directed to speak with a lady seated near the rear of the hall. Her mother was insistent that I spoke with her daughter and provided such substantial evidence of her survival that the daughter, Tina, subsequently phoned me at my home. During the phone call Tina's mother instantly drew close, and she showed me a beautiful array of violets, starting to rub my left ear as though she was trying to comfort me in some way. Tina confirmed that her mother's name was Violet, and at that time her left ear was so sore she had been using drops to ease the discomfort. At that point Tina arranged a private sitting and once again as soon as the sitting commenced, Tina's mother made her presence known to me.

Violet spoke about three crosses, added that she was aware that Tina was wearing the cross, and that she was right to take it. That comment appeared to provide an element of relief as Tina had been concerned about whether taking the cross had been the correct decision to make. It appears that Tina had given her mother a gold chain and cross as a present, and that Violet had worn the necklace until the end of her life. When Violet was taken from the funeral parlour to the church, Tina had removed the chain as a keepsake. Tina's mother then went on to talk about a second cross, using my hands I was directed to make the sign of a cross, wide and low across my chest. I asked Tina if this particular cross had been made out of lavender and she confirmed that as her mother lay in her coffin, using stems of fresh lavender, she had made a large cross and placed it gently on her chest. Violet then told me about a third cross, not the one that was previously mentioned but one that Tina had recently acquired and had on her that day. Tina was delighted as only that day one of her sisters had given her a cross and chain, but as she was already wearing her mother's she had put the other chain in her handbag. Violet was an excellent communicator and she went on to give relevant detailed evidence that provided Tina with the assurance she needed to know that her mother had indeed survived into the Spirit world.

During another public performance at the Beau Sejour Centre in Guernsey, a young man presented himself. He told me that he had taken his own life in prison. As he spoke, I felt a tremendous pressure around my neck as if I had burn marks cutting into my skin. He told me how he hated the confined space and was eventually unable to handle the harassment he received in prison. He added that his father was in the audience and he just needed him to know how sorry he was for the pain he had caused but that he was now at peace. He was aware that the court case was not settled and said that eventually all would come to light. At that point a man seated in the audience raised his hand; it was obvious from the tears that were streaming down his cheeks that he was acknowledging his son. At one stage I had to check if I should continue with the message, as I was being given some quite private and personal information. Eventually we brought the message to an end with the assurance that we would speak in private.

At times it is necessary to be discreet; sometimes even at a public demonstration you have to gauge what should and should not be repeated. I try to remember the relevance of the messages and the significant impact a particular message can have. The vulnerability of the audience members is a point I try never to forget. My focus is to try to relate a message in a dignified and respectable manner to both the communicator in Spirit and the person that is receiving the message. Often some of the details can be near the mark but they are given in ways that are accepted in good humour for the simple reason they show the true character of the person giving the evidence.

One such message was provided by a delightful young man. I was returning from one of my many trips to Ireland when I was greeted by a neighbour who commented about the sadness of a boy who had been killed in Iraq. I had not had the opportunity to keep up with the news as my schedule had been rigid and hectic, and it was a relief to arrive home. My thoughts were focused on kicking off my shoes, putting up my feet and having a much deserved cup of tea. No sooner had I sat down than the telephone rang, and as the lady began to speak, a young soldier drew close pleading with me to see his mother. He emphasised how concerned he was, so I naturally suggested she called around to see me in the next half hour.

The moment this lady stepped through the door, a very good-looking young man presented himself. He had a lovely sense of humour, he was full of laughter with an amazing smile that could have lit the darkest of rooms. For a moment he became serious and told me that he had been a fatality of the Iraq war when the helicopter he was being transported in had crashed, killing all on board. He told me to tell his mother that he had got his angel wings and that he could fly. He continued to provide his mother with personal information so that when she left she had a look of pure amazement that she did not have when she arrived. Four days later, the young man's body came back home and was buried with full military honours.

Some time later, the young man appeared before me for a second time; he was concerned that new information had come to light and about the effect it was to have on his mother. He wanted her to know that the news she was about to receive should bear no relevance on how he was now. He was insistent that she be reminded that his passing was instantaneous, that he felt no pain but had simply walked from one world to another. He smiled and added, *"Tell my mum I'm okay, I've got my willy"*.

Unsure of how to express myself in the right manner, I was reminded of one of the first lessons I learnt when I was developing. It is not my work to choose what should be passed on; don't add to or detract from what Spirit tell you, simply relay the message as it is given. I phoned his mother, who roared with laughter, acknowledging that it was exactly the kind of comment her son would have made. Had I altered what he had said to me, I would not have been doing my job properly. By speaking his exact words, his mother was assured that the message really came from her son.

Little did we know the true relevance of such an innocent comment. When the news arrived, it couldn't have been more distressing. It seems that other parts of the young man's body had been located in the shell of the helicopter. With confirmation of DNA results, his body was later exhumed. By warning his mother she was able to keep the situation in perspective. She had proof that her son was at peace, and whilst the news was immensely painful, the ability to cope was made that bit easier. Eighteen months later this young man appeared to me again, when he asked me to tell his mum that he had got the dog and was looking after his dad. On phoning his mother, she informed me that both her husband and the family dog had also passed.

On many occasions, I hear from people as a direct result of other sittings. Renée contacted me after reading an article in the Psychic News about the evidence given to Tina of the lavender cross in the coffin.

Renée had also lost her son tragically, and he had left behind a loving wife and two daughters. As soon as the telephone link was made, Renée's son drew close. He, too, was concerned about the effect his passing would have on his family. To prove his survival, he gave evidence of items placed in his coffin together with personal information. He told them he was aware that the doors of the church had been left open as so many people attended his funeral. He confirmed that a friend had also passed in the same manner as he had. He acknowledged that an enquiry was still being held, leaving the family feeling unsettled. Renée went on to have a number of sittings, and on these occasions she was provided with relevant details that convinced her of her son's survival.

That is the essence of my work. When I first realised my ability to communicate with Spirit, it opened my eyes to a whole new world of possibilities and filled me with awe. I had to know what was happening to me. I deepened my understanding of all matters Spiritual and shifted my focus to concentrate on proving the survival of Spirit. I became hungry to explore its meaning and implications; however, it is those who receive the messages that are able to express the true relevance of the evidence that Spirit provides for and through me.

Chapter 10

Summing Up

"Love thine enemies": it's not easy to forgive, let alone to love - this is our learning curve on Earth. This is to enable our God to bring love into our souls, because to allow us to progress we have to learn to forgive and to love. Life is a journey of gaining experience from this world to enable us to enter into the next.

I have positive personal proof of life after so-called death. The other side of life is the most wonderful place, where we are greeted by our loved ones to the sound of beautiful angelic music, which really is out of this world. The place is so tranquil; peace, love and contentment are truly something to behold. We meet with those we loved in the past, and the love of God is ever there, and with us. Our God loves us for who we are; for all our mistakes, we are still children of God. Again I stress we are always met by a caring Spirit when we move on in life; often a loved one who has been waiting for the correct time and is usually felt and seen at the departing person's side or nearby. It is a truly wonderful thought that we are not, and never will be alone, and we have no need to fear, for as the door of our new life opens so we start to live again free of pain, sorrow, hurt and sadness as we go to a home of peace. When I entered the spirit world many years ago, there were wonderful colours beyond belief and the love I felt made it hard to return to this world. To see your loved ones healthy again is a joy beyond anything else.

I do not fear death, for the very reason that I know we can't die. We live on - it is only our body that ceases to exist. At the moment of death, when the earthly person is ready or the spirit is ready for them, someone from the higher realms always comes to guide them to the next stage. In the same way as I experienced, they will feel such love, warmth and beauty that they are at ease and there is no fear. Sometimes a family member is afraid that perhaps their dying loved one will try to hang onto their earthly existence. Let them be assured no-one passes over afraid; before the exact time of passing they are shown such a peace that is often mirrored in their recognition of a higher life. The doors then open to the higher life; there are many levels in the spirit world and soon we progress to our rightful place, where we are available to give help to our loved ones still on earth, and naturally to be there to help them over when it is their time to join us. I strongly believe in the joy of reunion with one another when we enter the world of Spirit.

I say again and again that this was the greatest gift I could have been given; I had no doubts, no fear, all was well, my son who had passed was strong and perfect, my Gran was back to the beauty she had always been. In fact, this was proof of survival. *My mind accepted this vision, yet it was not what was wanted of me;* ***that was not my time.***

It is up to us to learn the lessons of earth, and progress to a higher realm for our new life, with no pain, no fear, no suffering and no worry of growing old in the future. We are lucky to have this to look forward to in time. And what is time? Time is an eternal interlude between one world and the next. This is our chance to learn the lessons we need to know for the progression of our soul to a higher life. One thing for certain is that the next life can't be as bad as the hurts and problems of this one; to me, this life at the moment is as near as possible to what we think hell will be.

When a mother is told her son has died; or her much loved child has been abused; or a dear husband suffers whilst awaiting death, surely that is hell? How can one bear the thoughts of our children in a War that we have not asked for, or a child that has been born deformed, or the loss of a baby? This is a path we have to walk to gain the wisdom of life. These are extremely hard lessons, and Mary, Mother of Jesus, must have felt that pain; yet she had her faith, saying *"God's will be done."* Oh! If only we were as strong.

I know the world we call Heaven is there at the end of our earthly lives. We are not judged by earthly standards, but are welcomed by a much higher realm. I know the world of love is there to enable us to grow into better people. If we love each other as the Bible says, then we forgive. I hope I would be worthy in those circumstances, for I think I would have great difficulty in forgiving if it were my dear ones that had been harmed or murdered.

How can we love someone who abuses vulnerable people, or wicked tyrants who threaten our children? No way! We are human, and I am certainly no saint; as I have often said with regard to my own children, I would want to retaliate if someone caused such pain. I am a human being with human thoughts and feelings, and there are times when in my ignorance I say to God, *"Why did you let that happen? Why must the good suffer?"* Then I remind myself that God gave us 'Free Will' to choose; and this is the greatest gift he has given to mankind.

At the time of passing to a higher life, all of our deeds are known to God, and he does not greet us with the fires of hell. Our Father God loves each and every one of us and he accepts all our faults. I believe that we judge ourselves; for who knows us better than ourselves!

Words are not the only way Spirit communicates. The true spirit communication is 'mind talk' and often we might 'hear' our name called or suchlike, yet it is not always so. Spirit does not need a voice box, in the same way that they do not need a body. This is often shown to us to help us to understand and grasp who Spirit is. Communicators work on the vibration energy, and it is often the Trance Medium who can be heard. This is when the Spirit uses the voice box of the Trance Medium; there are few mediums generally with this ability. Spirit are very particular who they work with, and it is of paramount importance for the energies to blend. Communication is likened to an electric energy to the human brain and the awareness of the individual. We are sometimes shown bodily forms to make it easier for us to accept; at other times a familiar thought crosses the mind; or a special tune; the smell of their favourite tobacco smoke; even a perfume which the loved one used to wear. Dismiss none of these sensations, for they are awareness, and need to be remembered.

I myself could not understand the purpose or the urgency of my second book. I was in a whirl; I came to a complete stop; everything seemed to be against it. Lost paperwork, missing chapters, a delay in typing, and my reaction was to think: *"Oh s** it why am I bothered, it certainly won't help my finances, probably I will lose out, that's the story of my life"*.

In the beginning when I asked myself, *"Why bother?"* I also asked Spirit the same question, and I was told the purpose of the book is to *"dispel fear of the life to come, and help others to know, as you know, that you cannot die. The soul is eternal; the spirit is the energy that is also eternal."*

I felt that this second book was taking far too long to write, and there had been so many hiccups along the way. For example, I lost the typed manuscript, my computer kept crashing every ten days or so, and I genuinely worried if it was worth trying as I certainly have gained little from my first book, which cost me a fortune to produce. I seemed to give so many of those away, but then I realised that my rewards have been from people who have come to me and said that it made their understanding of passing over easier, and that because I speak straight from the heart with simple words, most people can understand and find comfort.

Lack of money did not allow for me to use someone else to do most of the work typing up the second book, so I carried on in my own clumsy way. And I repeat, again, I asked Spirit *"Why do you want this new book?"* and, by golly, was I told, yet again. This book you are reading now, which almost never was, exists to dispel fear, to enable ordinary people like yourself and myself to understand that the life to come is nothing to fear; for when we enter that time, there is no more pain, no more loneliness. People can go, can pass on, knowing that tomorrow is to be another day, and that one day we will all be together again.

I had been working on this book, and had come to a standstill; then, yet again, I was very ill. I was diagnosed with serious cancer of the kidney. I was quickly admitted to hospital. It looked as though I would never finish this book; Spirit hadn't even given me the title.

Three days before going into hospital I vowed that if my second chance was there I would be more considerate to the people I love; my husband, my children and all the family. I went to bed with these thoughts strongly in my mind. Two nights before I was admitted to hospital, I dozed and suddenly I was aware of a strange feeling within me and a sense of confusion. I found myself in my own bedroom, yet it was not mine; what I was seeing was a very tidy room, with none of my junk around, which was certainly strange, since I am a very untidy person who lives in clutter!

I heard my sons talking to their Dad; they were talking about me. My reaction was '*what on earth is going on, what have they done with my stuff, where are my perfumes, where are all my books from the side of the bed?'* I distinctly saw my son go to the wardrobe and take out a jacket I am very fond of; he said, *"We can't give this away, Mum loved it."* I tried to make them understand that I was listening, I even shouted at them, my thoughts were *'Have they all gone deaf, do they think I am dead!'*

That was it. Spirit were showing me what it is like to feel frustrated and to need to communicate. My Guide then appeared; I must admit I wasn't very sociable, and I said *"that was cruel wasn't it"?* To which my answer came *"We gave you back this world to give understanding of Spirit to others; now we say to you explain to others the frustrations for us when earth people will not listen to the Spirit word".*

My guide smiled and said *"Dear One, your family* ***know*** *of the after-life, imagine how difficult it is for those who have no knowledge, only fear, of Spirit."*

What a major lesson, to be sure.

The day of my hospital admission came, and I looked at my home with different eyes. I realized what I had taken for granted over the years - sometimes we need something like the word 'cancer' to make us understand our vulnerability. Then we were on our way, me with the new nighties and posh deodorants and a good supply of underwear in my suitcase - after all, it is best to be prepared!

I was up-tight. If I said anything different it would be a lie. On arrival at the hospital I was given an X-Ray, blood tests, water tests - you name it, they tested it - and then I was given a drip. This was because I was taking the drug Warfarin to keep my blood from clotting, following my heart surgery many years ago. John, my husband, was with me and he was tired of waiting around. When a midday meal was served up – well, say no more, John went to find the canteen and bought both of us some chips, and we ate them in the Day Room.

I soon became used to seeing patients walking around with tubes connected to them. The doctor came to see me, saying they were waiting for a bed as there had been a change in someone being discharged. It was around five o'clock in the afternoon and I was told, *"Sorry, no bed, you will have to go home and come back tomorrow, and you will have to be connected to the drip you have overnight."*

The stubborn side of me came out – *"Oh, no! I am not travelling in a car with this stuck out of the roof like an aerial!"* They did see the funny side; I felt like crying, yet I stuck to my guns and said *"I would rather stay in the Day room all night"*. They were still phoning around for a bed for me for the night. I sent a prayer up, and within five minutes a doctor came along the ward, and he asked what the problem was. He turned to me and said *"Don't worry you can have the Emergency bed in my ward."* I sent my thanks to God, and I could have hugged that doctor. He had come on the ward purely by chance for something else. John, poor lad, returned home, I do believe very tired and strained. (Perhaps I don't always say to him what I should, yet I do say with all my heart that he is one in a million.) I had as comfortable a night as could be expected with a drip in my hand, until I was weaned off the Warfarin I could not have my first operation. It took numerous tests and blood tests and many drips before I was ready.

The first operation was to cut off the blood supply from my cancerous kidney to enable it to be shrunk. Oh, did I feel ill, and when I came around all my family were there. I could see their fear and my heart went out to them; then I fell asleep again. Later, I awoke to see a wonderful glow at the bottom of my bed; there stood my Mum and Dad, my special friend Jim, my guide, and a dark gentleman who said his name was John, (and it wasn't my husband) looking so kindly at me. I was receiving healing. I looked to the side of me and there, all hazy, stood a friend Jim, of the earth; I felt his healing energy coming toward me. The dark man smiled at him, and I remember my guide saying to me "*You have asked many times, daughter, the name of the second book. I give it to you now. 'A Little More Time'*". Two days later, the next operation was a much easier one. I came back from surgery minus one kidney and one tumour; yes, I do have that '*Little More Time*'.

That was in March 2006; now it is ten months on, I am still working for Spirit, and I do believe I am wiser in many ways. Thanks to the wonderful skills of my very special surgeon and the successful operation, my husband and I were able to celebrate our Golden Wedding Anniversary in October 2006, along with family and friends, which made the celebration all the more special.

All the Churches and colleagues sent out their prayers, and the love that has wrapped around me, from my dear husband, my family and friends, all their love and support has been enormous. I have much to be grateful for in my friends of a higher Spiritual level and earthly level. Good wishes came from all over the world; I received 275 Get Well cards. This is 'Margaret the Person' - with 'A Little More Time' to give.

I am indebted to the hospital Staff and have started making preparations for a number of Fundraising Evenings (together with people who have already benefited from this life-saving operation) commencing in 2007 for a Kidney Cancer Unit that is badly needed in North Wales to benefit those who find they are unfortunate to be diagnosed with Kidney Cancer. Therefore, ensuring hope and trying to give the needy 'A Little More Time'.

Appendix

Out of the Dark Ages

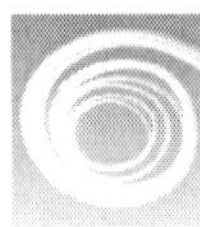

A brief synopsis of the first pioneering mediums and proponents of Spiritualism without whom my work would have been made considerably more difficult.

The Fox Sisters

On December 11th, 1847, John D. Fox secured the tenancy of a house in Hydesville, New York, USA. This small hamlet located twenty miles from Rochester, New York was the location generally considered as the birthplace of the modern spiritualist movement. John Fox and his wife Margaret together with two of their daughters Kate (Cathie) and Margaretta (Margaret) moved into the house after the previous tenant, Mr. Michael Weakman chose to vacate the premises following the manifestation of what he could only describe as inexplicable forces. At first, the family experienced no disturbances, but that all changed in the spring of 1848. In March of that year they started to hear noises that sounded like knocks and raps, together with what appeared to be the sound of moving furniture. The children were so shaken by these experiences they refused to be alone in the house. On March 31st there was an increase in activity; it was a particularly windy night and after Mrs Fox suggested the source of the noises may have come from the window sashes, Mr. Fox attempted to shake the sashes to see if they had become loose. It was at that point that Kate Fox noticed that every time her father shook the window sashes the noises echoed the exact sound seconds later. Kate Fox was unaware that her actions were about to make history. By snapping her fingers she challenged the unseen forces to respond. The following account is the official testimony of events as presented in *"A Report of the Mysterious Noises heard in the House of Mr. John D. Fox."* This is a pamphlet containing Mr and Mrs Fox's statements taken by E. E. Lewis, Esq. of Canandaigua published at Canandaigua, New York in 1848.

"On the night of the first disturbance we all got up, lighted a candle and searched the entire house, the noises continuing during this time and being heard near the same place. Although not very loud, it produced a jar of the bedsteads and chairs that could be felt when we were in bed. It was a tremulous motion, more than a sudden jar . We could feel the jar when standing on the floor. It continued on this night until we slept. I did not sleep until about twelve o'clock. On March 30 we were disturbed all night. The noises were heard in all parts of the house. My husband stationed himself outside the door while I stood inside, and the knocks came on the door between us. We heard footsteps in the pantry, and walking downstairs; we could not rest, and then I concluded that the house must be haunted by some unhappy restless spirit. I had often heard of such things, but I had never witnessed anything of the kind that I could not account for before.

On Friday night, March 31st, 1848, we concluded to go to bed early and not permit ourselves to be disturbed by the noises, but try and get a night's rest. My husband was here on all these occasions, heard the noises and helped in the search. It was very early when we went to bed on this night, hardly dark. I had been so broken of my rest I was almost sick. My husband had not gone to bed when we first heard the noise on this evening. I had just lain down. It commenced as usual. I knew it from all the other noises I had ever heard before, the children who slept in the other bed in the room, heard the rapping and tried to make similar sounds by snapping their fingers.

My youngest child, Cathie, said, 'Mr Splitfoot, do as I do,' clapping her hands. The sound instantly followed her with the same number of raps. When she stopped the sound ceased for a short time. Then Margaretta said, in sport, 'No, do just as I do. Count one, two, three, four,' striking one hand against the other at the same time; and the raps came as before. She was afraid to repeat them. Then Cathie said in her childish simplicity, 'Oh mother, I know what it is. Tomorrow is April fool day and it is somebody trying to fool us.'

'I then thought I could put a test that no one in the place could answer. I asked the noise to rap my different children's ages, successfully, instantly each one of my children's ages was given correctly, pausing between them sufficiently long to individualise them until the seventh, at which a longer pause was made, and then three more emphatic raps were given, corresponding to the little one that died, which was my youngest child.'

'I then asked, 'Is this a human being that answers my questions so correctly? 'There was no rap. I asked 'Is it a spirit? If it is make two raps,' which were instantly made. Two sounds were given as soon as the request was made. I then said, 'If it was an injured spirit, make two raps, which were instantly made, causing the house to tremble. I asked, 'Were you injured in this house? The answer was given as before. 'Is the person living that injured you? Answered by raps, in the same manner. I ascertained by the same simple method that it was a man, aged 31 years, that he had been murdered in this house and his remains were buried in the cellar; that his family consisted of a wife and five children, two sons and three daughters, all living at the time of his death, but that the wife had since died. I asked, 'Will you continue to rap if I call my neighbours that they may

hear it too? The raps were loud in the affirmative'.

'My husband went and called in Mrs Redfield, our nearest neighbour. She is a very candid woman. The girls were sitting up in bed clinging to each other and trembling with terror. I think I was as calm as I am now. Mrs Redfield came immediately (this was about half past seven), thinking she would have a laugh at the children. But when she saw them pale with fright and nearly speechless, she was amazed and believed there was something more serious than she had supposed. I asked a few questions for her and she was answered as before. He told her age exactly. She then called her husband, and the same questions were asked and answered.'

'Then Mr. Redfield called in Mr. Duesler and wife, and several others. Mr. Duesler then called in Mr. and Mrs. Hyde, also Mr. and Mrs Jewel Mr Duesler asked many questions and received answers. I then named all the neighbours I could think of and asked if any of them had injured him and received no answer. Mr Duesler then asked questions and received answers. He asked, 'Were you murdered? Raps affirmative. 'Can your murderer be brought to justice? No sound. 'Can he be punished by law? No answer. He then said, 'If your murderer cannot be punished by the law manifest it by raps,' and the raps were made clearly and distinctly. In the same way Mr. Duesler ascertained that he was murdered in the east bedroom about five years ago and that the murder was committed by a Mr.?, on a Tuesday night at twelve o'clock, that he was murdered by having his throat cut with a butcher's knife; that the body was taken through the buttery, down the stairway and that it was buried ten feet below the surface of the ground. It was also ascertained that he was murdered for his money by raps affirmative.' 'How much was it, one hundred? No rap. 'Was it two hundred?' etc., and when he mentioned five hundred the raps replied in the affirmative.'

'Many called in who were fishing in the creek, and all heard the same questions and answers. Many remained in the

house all night. I and my children left the house. My husband remained in the house with Mr. Redfield all night. On the next Saturday the house was filled to overflowing. There were no sounds heard during the day, but they commenced again in the evening. It was said that there was over three hundred persons present at the time. On Sunday morning the noises were heard throughout the day by all who came to the house.'

'On Saturday night, April 1st, they commenced digging in the cellar; they dug until they came to water and then gave it up. The noise was not heard on Sunday evening nor during the night. Stephen B. Smith and wife (my daughter Marie) and my son David S. Fox and wife, slept in the room this night. I have heard nothing since that time until yesterday there were several questions answered in way by rapping. I have heard the noise several times today.'

'I am not a believer in haunted houses or supernatural appearances. I am very sorry there has been so much excitement about it. It has been a great deal of trouble to us. It was our misfortune to live here at this time; but I am willing and anxious that the truth should be known and that a true statement should be made. I cannot account for these noises; all that I know is that they have been heard repeatedly as I have stat. d. I have heard this rapping again this (Tuesday) morning, April 4. My children have also heard it.'

'I certify that the foregoing statement has been read to me and that the same is true; and that I should be willing to take my oath that it is so if necessary.'

April 11, 1848. (Signed) Margaret Fox.

It is understood that the rapping noises continued until the body was located. Although the Fox sisters became established mediums in their own right, later joined by a third sister, Leah, the sisters were always remembered and connected to the events that took place in Hydesville that evening of March 31st, 1848.

Andrew Jackson Davis

In another New York hamlet by the name of Blooming Grove, located alongside the Hudson River, Andrew Jackson Davis was born to poverty-stricken parents. His father earned a pittance as a shoemaker and weaver and succumbed to alcoholism, leaving his family destitute. As a child Andrew Davis showed early signs of his clairvoyant ability, hearing voices at an age when such instances were considered by him to be a natural process. Born in 1826, by the time he was twelve years of age he had proved his ability to the extent that on the advice of Spirit he convinced his father to move the family to Poughkeepsie in 1838. This was to be a significant move as five years later when Andrew Davis was just seventeen years old he started to attend a series of lectures on mesmerism. A later meeting with a Mr. William Levingston helped reduce Andrew Davis to a state of mesmeric trance. In this altered state of consciousness he was able to accurately diagnose other people's medical disorders. He would describe how he could locate and see those organs that were diseased. His accuracy became widely known; the combination of spirit communication and trance medium-ship were to propel him to great fame and is to this day still referred to as the John the Baptist of modern spiritualism.

Emma Hardinge Britten

Emma Hardinge Britten is still considered to be a major proponent and pioneer of American spiritualism, her classic publication, 'Modern American Spiritualism' is today referred to as the most complete account of the American movement. Dedicated to spreading the word of spirit communication she travelled extensively throughout the United States, Canada, New Zealand, Australia and England. Born in England in 1823, she travelled to America in 1856 as part of a theatrical company, a gifted musician and vocalist she met with a Mrs Coan who instilled in her an intrigue for all matters spiritual. She began developing her own abilities, these ranged from psychometry to automatic and inspirational writing to healing. In trance she was controlled by a member of the crew of the steamer 'Pacific' that had sunk disclosing the facts before the boat owners had made the details public knowledge. She was threatened with prosecution by the owners, but the case never made it to the courts as the information was found to be accurate. Her dream of establishing a training school for mediums was realised the year after her death when the Britten Memorial institute and library was founded in Manchester, England. As founder and editor of the 'Two Worlds' magazine that is still published bi- monthly in the United Kingdom, she was also among the founders of the Theosophical Society of New York, although she was quick to denounce any connections with Madam Blavatsky.

Florence Cook

Florence Cook was regarded as one of the most famous physical mediums of her age. Extensively researched by Sir William Crookes her ability was first recognised after she attended materialisation sittings with notable mediums of the day, Herne and Williams. At one point she withdrew from giving sittings as the materialisations became too strong for her to handle. Sadly her career was cut short when she died at the tender age of forty eight.

Helena Petrovna Blavatsky

Helena Petrovna Blavatsky was the founder of the Theosophical Society; throughout her sixty years she maintained a passion for spiritual communications. Despite her dedication to her beliefs she was at times more renowned for her unusual behaviour that clouded people's perception of her. There is no doubt she was genuinely gifted, her insight was unique, her determination at that point unrivalled. Born in 1831, the daughter of Colonel Peter Hahn, a Russian officer, she was raised in an atmosphere of superstition. Her fantasies remained an integral part of her character, which played a substantial role in diminishing her credibility.

Mrs Leonore E. Piper

Mrs Piper was considered to be the most respected trance medium of her era. She was a highly regarded individual, her honesty and integrity above reproach. She married William Piper of Boston in 1879 and all reference to her indicates that she was forever referred to by her married name and rarely by her given name Leonore. At the age of eight, when playing at her home she felt a blow to her right ear; on hearing the words 'Aunt Sara, not dead, but with you still,' she ran terrified to her mother's side. Some time later it was discovered that Aunt Sara had died at that exact time. Not wishing to alarm the child any further her mediumistic abilities were discouraged until such time she was of age. Soon after her marriage she attended a development circle where she would instantly fall into trance. Her abilities strengthened and she maintained a credible career until her passing at the age of 93.

Eileen J. Garrett

Born in Beauparc County, Ireland in 1893, Eileen Garrett's early life was tainted by the tragic suicide of both of her parents. Raised by caring relatives she was to grow up accustomed to seeing spirit. As a respected and talented medium she began her quest to research and understand paranormal phenomena. She recognised the need for an open minded but scientific investigation in to all that she had come to know and understand. Her journey was to research, write accounts, publish and lecture her findings. Her contributions remain highly respected by scientists and mediums alike.

Sir Arthur Conan Doyle

Born on May 22nd, 1859, to a prosperous Irish Catholic family, his father was Charles Altamont Doyle, a chronic alcoholic, and his mother was Mary Doyle an accomplished storyteller. It was his mother's love for writing that influenced his career. Sir Arthur Ignatius Conan Doyle is mainly renowned for his 'Sherlock Holmes' novels. A prolific writer of his times his passion for matters spiritual was born when his father passed away without giving him the chance to settle a basic misunderstanding. His search led him to attend sittings at the home of one of his patients, General Drayson, whilst working as a physician in Southsea. He went on to join the 'Society of Psychical Research', and continued his research for over thirty years collaborating with such eminent colleagues as Sir Oliver Lodge. At the peak of his literary career it was his interest in spiritualism that dominated his work, his association with modern spiritualism became his priority, his publications became classics and are constantly referred to by all those who have followed in his footsteps.

Sir Oliver Lodge

Sir Oliver was a world renowned physicist. His belief in human survival was to dominate much of his research. His passion to prove survival by scientific methods was to gain him undisputed respect from colleagues and strangers alike; this was not always the case as initially he joined the Society of Psychical Research because he had found a series of evidence that he considered neglected by scientists. He had a belief that messages could be transferred and received in much the same way as mediums connect with spirit, his dedicated research led him to become a pioneer in wireless telegraphy and actually sent a radio message one year before Marconi. On arrival at the headquarters of the Spiritualist Association of Great Britain in Belgrave Square, London, you are greeted with two life size portraits, one of Sir Oliver, the other Sir Arthur Conan Doyle. Much of their work enabled the society to buy the building in which they still remain housed. Sir Oliver's lifetime achievements remain evident to all who have a basic understanding of Spiritualism.

Helen Duncan

Helen Duncan was a physical medium; under the right conditions she had the ability to produce ectoplasm that would form the appearance of those who had long since passed to spirit. She was arrested in 1944 and imprisoned in Holloway Gaol, London, convicted under the 1735 Witchcraft Act. Following her trial, the law was abolished and replaced in 1951 by The Fraudulent Mediums Act. Britain's Prime Minister at the time, Winston Churchill was infuriated by the case and his feelings paved the way for the reform. Born Victoria Helen Mcfarlane on November 25th, 1898, in Callander, Perthshire, she was an uneducated women and mother of nine children, three of whom died in childbirth. It is a commonly held belief that Mrs Duncan was arrested not because she was allegedly fraudulent, but because she had revealed details of the sinking of HMS Barham before the Ministry of Defence had made the details public knowledge. Twelve years later the police authorities interrupted another of her sittings; at the time it is said she was producing ectoplasm, which instantly shot back into her body causing burns and severe shock. Six weeks later Helen Duncan died supposedly of diabetes and heart failure; those who knew her blamed the police for her treatment, which today many people believe accounted for her death.

Doris Stokes

Doris Stokes is without doubt the most internationally renowned medium of all time. On May 8th, 1986, Doris passed to the spirit world leaving a void that has never been replaced. Doris was unique in that her down to earth nature enabled her to reach more individuals than any other medium has done before or since. She was the first medium to capture the public's imagination, and her series of autobiographical books became best selling publications. Despite this success she never sought financial gain, as most of her royalties were given to charity. She had the ability to touch the hearts of people all over the world; she travelled extensively throughout the United Kingdom, America and Australia. As a clairaudient, she was able to provide extensive survival evidence; her accuracy was consistent, her dedication unparalleled. Throughout her life she was plagued with ill health and suffered the tragedy of losing her son, John Michael. Her beloved father appeared to her on several occasions, and he forewarned that her son was to return to spirit. She was devastated at the news and threw herself into her work; after numerous miscarriages she and her beloved husband John adopted a son, Terry. Within a few years of her passing both her husband and son also passed to spirit. I can only imagine what a reunion they must have had when the entire family were finally reunited!

Other Productions
by Margaret Hurdman

Margaret has produced two CDs which are designed and created to help you meditate.

Time to Relax - Comprising Tracks

Indian Village
The Beach
Who is my Angel
The Doors

A Time to Dream - Comprising Tracks

Mountain
Pegasus
The Forest
Nature Spirits

For more information and to listen to samples of these tracks please log on to Margarets website

w: www.margarethurdman.co.uk

or contact Margaret directly by email

e: margaretmedium@btopenworld.com

Other Productions
by Margaret Hurdman

Margaret's Second Book:

A Little More Time

Further copies of this book can be ordered directly from: Margaret, the publishers, online bookstores and most book shops in the UK

£8.99
ISBN 13: 978-1-905930-02-9

Publisher: Porto Publishing
w: www.portopublishing.com
w: www.margarethurdman.co.uk
e: margaretmedium@btopenworld.com

Margaret's First Book:

Margaret The Person - Living a Spirited Life

Can be ordered directly from: Margaret, the publishers, online bookstores and most book shops in the UK

£6.50
ISBN 10: 1-904440-52-5
ISBN 13: 978-1-904440-52-9

Publisher: Librario Publishing Ltd
w: www.librario.com
w: www.margarethurdman.co.uk
e: margaretmedium@btopenworld.com